Kickoff Upgrade
Workbook

von
David Christie

Ernst Klett Verlag
Stuttgart · Leipzig

Kickoff Upgrade

Workbook mit Lösungsheft

Autor: David Christie, Oxford

Werkübersicht:

Kickoff Foundation Schülerbuch, 978-3-12-808295-0
Kickoff Foundation Workbook mit Lösungsheft, 978-3-12-808303-2
Kickoff Upgrade Schülerbuch, 978-3-12-808296-7
Kickoff Upgrade Workbook mit Lösungsheft, 978-3-12-808304-9
Kickoff Lehrerhandbuch inkl. Digitalem Lehrer-Service mit Medien-DVD-ROM + Lehrer-Audio-CDs (2), 978-3-12-808305-6

1. Auflage 1 5 4 3 2 1 | 18 17 16 15 14

Redaktion: Gaby Bauer-Negenborn, Weßling
Herstellung: Sarah Ganser

Satz und Gestaltung: Satzkiste, Stuttgart
Umschlaggestaltung: KOMA AMOK, Kunstbüro für Gestaltung, Stuttgart
Reproduktion: Meyle + Müller Medien-Management, Pforzheim
Druck: Druckhaus Götz GmbH, Ludwigsburg

Printed in Germany
ISBN 978-3-12-808304-9

9 783128 083049

Unit 1 Tomorrow's world (Ss-Buch: /) 4

Grammar 4
Vocabulary 6
Writing 7
Video lounge 8

Unit 2 Travelling for work (Ss-Buch: Unit 2) 9

Grammar 9
Vocabulary 10
Writing 11
Video lounge 13

Unit 3 Apprenticeships (Ss-Buch: Unit 6) 14

Grammar 14
Vocabulary 15
Writing 16
Video lounge 18

Unit 4 A visit to a company (Ss-Buch: Unit 3) 19

Grammar 19
Vocabulary 21
Writing 22
Video lounge 23

Unit 5 Global business (Ss-Buch: Unit 4) 24

Grammar 24
Vocabulary 26
Writing 27
Video lounge 28

Unit 6 A month in New Zealand (Ss-Buch: Unit 5) 29

Grammar 29
Vocabulary 31
Writing 32
Video lounge 33

Unit 7 My job is special (Ss-Buch: /) 34

Grammar 34
Vocabulary 36
Writing 38
Video lounge 38

Unit 8 Starting work (Ss-Buch: Unit 1) 39

Grammar 39
Vocabulary 41
Writing 42
Video lounge 43

Unit 9 Working in an office (Ss-Buch: /) 44

Grammar 44
Vocabulary 46
Writing 48
Video lounge 48

Anhang 49

Job pages 50
Vocabulary by themes 62

Unit 1 Tomorrow's world

Grammar

1 ***If*-sentences type 1. Match the sentence halves from the two lists below. Write out the complete sentences.**

1 If the weather is nice tomorrow,
2 I won't go out tomorrow
3 If I have enough money one day,
4 Your parents will be angry
5 I'll be really surprised
6 What will you do

a if Mike goes out with Carol.
b if it rains.
c if you don't clean your room.
d I'll go to the park.
e if you miss your train?
f I'll visit New York.

If-Sätze Typ 1

If-Sätze (auch Konditionalsätze genannt) erzählen, was passiert, falls etwas anderes geschieht. Sie bestehen aus zwei Teilen: dem *if*-Teil und dem Hauptsatz. In Sätzen vom Typ 1 steht im *if*-Teil immer das *simple present* und im Hauptsatz das *will future*. Beide Teile können auch verneint sein. Und der Satz kann entweder mit dem *if*-Teil beginnen oder mit dem Hauptsatz (mit *will*).
*If X **happens**, Y **will happen**.*
*Y **will happen** if X **happens**.*
*If X **doesn't happen**, Y **will happen**.*

2 ***If sentences* type 1. Finish the sentences in this short story with the correct forms – the *simple present* or the *will future*.**

time travellers: 200 000 million years ago

TAD AND HIS FRIEND MIKKO were at Tad's house. It was a Saturday afternoon in the year 2074. "Look here," said Tad. "On the information wall. There's an ad for a time holiday." "Those time holidays are *really* expensive," said Mikko. "If we **(1)** book (to book) this holiday today, it **(2)** 'll be (to be) half price," said Tad. "Come on, let's go for it!"

Two weeks later, Tad and Mikko were at the offices of *Time Holidays Inc.* There were 15 people in their group, and a young woman called Jodie. "Listen, please," said Jodie. "We'll leave for our time holiday in ten minutes. You'll visit the earth 200 million years ago – at the time of the dinosaurs. But first, there's one very, *very* important thing. You mustn't touch anything on your holiday." "Why?" asked Tad. "If you **(3)** ______ (to touch) anything," answered Jodie, "you **(4)** ______ (to change) the future. And if you **(5)** ______ (to change) the future, we **(6)** ______ (to come back) to a very different world after our holiday. OK. Is everybody ready? Let's go!"

Tad, Mikko and the other time travellers went into the time room with Jodie. There was a dazzling light*, then they were on earth 200 million years ago. "Wow!" said Mikko. "Look at those dinosaurs. They're enormous! If they **(7)** ______ (to come) near us, I **(8)** ______ (to run)!" "No," said Jodie. "We **(9)** ______ (to go) home if there **(10)** ______ (to be) a problem. Don't run. You absolutely must stay here on the path**. If you **(11)** ______ (to leave) the path, you **(12)** ______ (to touch) something, perhaps."

Two hours later, the time holiday was almost over. "Just one more thing," said Jodie. "If you **(13)** ______ (to look) over there, you **(14)** ______ (to see) ..."

But she didn't finish the sentence. Suddenly, a pterodactyl – an enormous, flying dinosaur – flew towards them. Tad fell to the ground. And he put his hand into the grass near the path. He looked at his hand. In it, there was a beautiful butterfly. Tad put the butterfly in his pocket. "I think we **(15)** ______ (to go) home now if you **(16)** ______ (to be) all ready," said Jodie. She took a small machine from her pocket, there was the dazzling light again, and then they were back on earth in the year 2074.

An hour later, Tad and Mikko were outside in the street. "I brought something back from the holiday," said Tad. He showed Mikko the butterfly. "You're crazy!" said Mikko. "Jodie said ..." "I know," answered Tad. "'You **(17)** ______ (to change) the future if you **(18)** ______ (to touch) anything.' But it's only a butterfly. And the world looks, well, normal. So there isn't a problem."

Just then, two dogs walked past. "Good morning," said one of the dogs. Tad and Mikko looked at the dog. "But you're a dog," said Tad. "You can't talk." "Of course we can talk," said the dog. "All dogs can talk. In fact, we're police dogs, and if you **(19)** ______ (to be) rude again, we **(20)** ______ (to arrest***) you!"

→ * dazzling light: *blendendes Licht* → ** path: *Fußweg* → *** to arrest sb: *jmdn verhaften*

Vocabulary

3 Try this crossword about the future. All the words were in the unit.

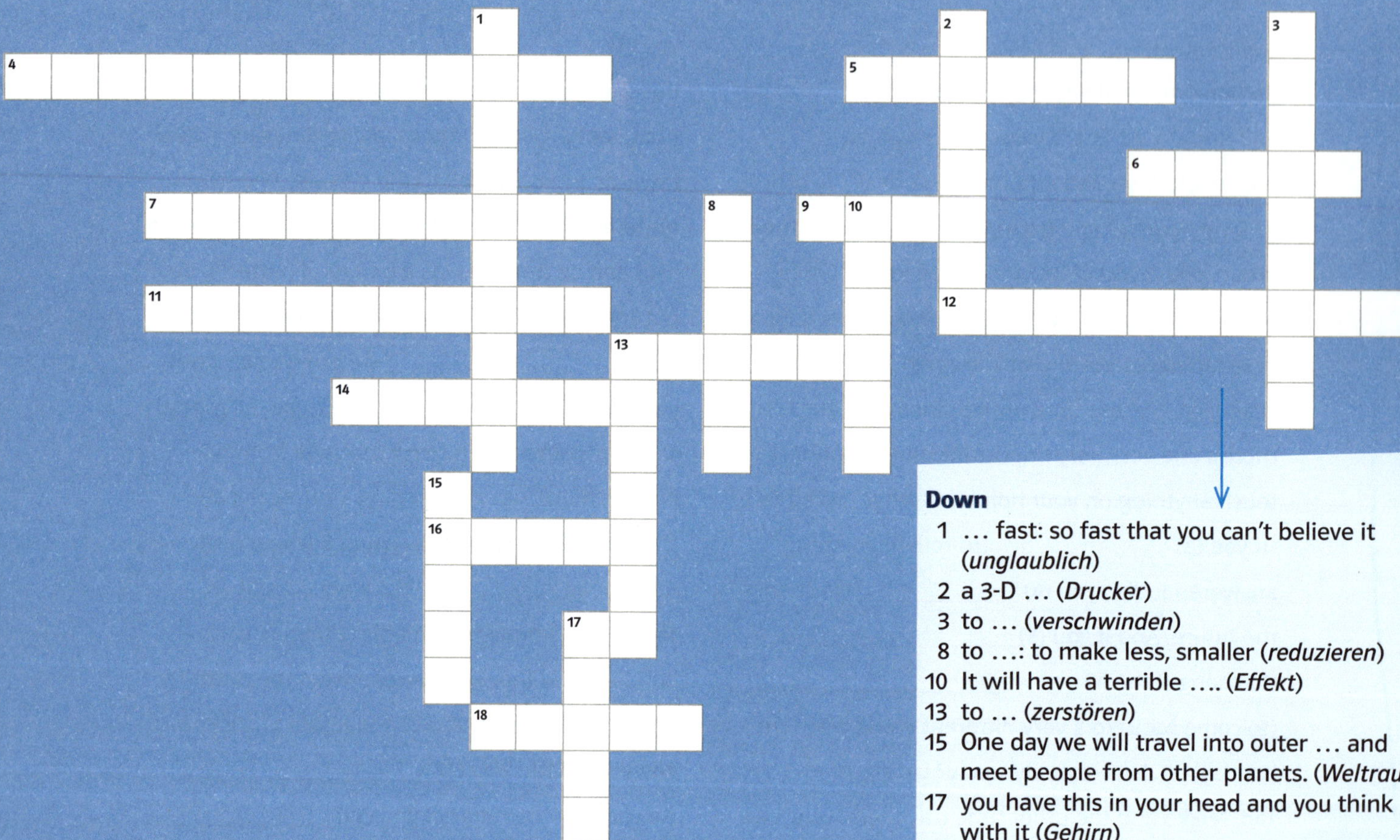

Down

1 … fast: so fast that you can't believe it (*unglaublich*)
2 a 3-D … (*Drucker*)
3 to … (*verschwinden*)
8 to …: to make less, smaller (*reduzieren*)
10 It will have a terrible …. (*Effekt*)
13 to … (*zerstören*)
15 One day we will travel into outer … and meet people from other planets. (*Weltraum*)
17 you have this in your head and you think with it (*Gehirn*)

Across

4 climate change (2 words)
5 … reality (*virtuell*)
6 … energy is energy from the sun
7 cars in the future won't use petrol, they will use … (*saubere Treibstoffe*) (2 words)
9 to … (*schmelzen*)
11 you are one of these (*Lebewesen*) (2 words)
12 a place with lots of trees e.g. in the Amazon (*Regenwald*)
13 to …: to become twice as big (*verdoppeln*)
14 to …: to look for new places (*erforschen*)
16 the … of computers (*Macht*)
17 … the year 2050 (*bis zu*)
18 extremely big (*riesig*)

4 Write in the opposites (*Gegenteile*) of the words.

1 better	worse	7 faster	
2 bright		8 near	
3 clean		9 rich	
4 cooler		10 smallest	
5 dangerous		11 to appear	
6 easy		12 virtual	

5 Using the word *unless*. Read the box on the right, then rewrite the sentences below with *unless*.

1 If we don't find new forms of clean energy, there will be more CO_2 in our atmosphere.

____

____

____

2 If we don't stop global warming, people in the poorer parts of the world will die of hunger.

____

____

____

> ***Unless***
>
> Das Wort unless bedeutet „wenn … nicht". Man kann es im *if*-Teil von verneinten Konditionalsätzen verwenden, um *if … not* zu ersetzen.
>
> ***If*** we ***don't reduce*** the CO_2 we produce, our atmosphere will become warmer.
>
> ***Unless*** we reduce the CO_2 we produce, our atmosphere will become warmer.

3 If our lives don't change, the future will be a disaster.

____

____

Writing

6 A good way to improve* your writing, is to learn to use some useful phrases. These words and phrases can connect *(verbinden)* short sentences together and they make your text more interesting.

1 Choose the best words and phrases in the list below to complete the sentences.
2 Write your own short text about the future. Use the words and phrases you used in the sentences. Write on a separate piece of paper.

also   and   but   for example   in fact   of course   that means that   too

a Robots will work on farms, in factories ____________________ in our homes.

b Robots will ____________________ drive cars and perhaps be police officers.

c They will do operations in hospitals, ____________________.

d 3-D printing is a new technology today ____________________ in the future it will become more and more important.

e ____________________, with 3-D printers, we will be able to make everything we need ourselves.

f The power of computers will double every one or two years. ____________________ by 2050, they will be able to do things we can't even imagine now.

g And, ____________________, the internet will be everywhere and incredibly fast.

h With virtual reality we will be able to 'be' in a situation – ____________________, to lie on a beach on a beautiful island.

→ *to improve: *verbessern*

Video lounge

7 Watching videos, films or TV in English is a great way to practise your listening skills. The more you do it, the easier it is to understand English when you hear it. Try, too, to learn some new words and phrases from what you hear – note them down and learn them. These words and phrases are often the ones you hear (and can then use) in everyday, spoken language.

1 Watch the video and read the dialogue below. Concentrate first on getting a *general understanding (grobes Verständnis)* of the dialogue.
2 Watch again and look at the underlined words and phrases.
Can you guess what they mean? Compare ideas in class, then use your dictionary to check.
3 Note down the words and phrases and learn them.

London, bistro

Maya Oh, hi, Josh! I know I'm late. I'm so sorry! I'm really, really sorry!

Josh Late? Thirty minutes is more than late, Maya. It's almost insulting.

Maya Nice work, Josh!

Josh I know you're working on your acting career, but a little less of the 'diva' would be nice sometimes.

Maya Oh, come on! The next coffee is on me.

Josh Thanks, but I've already had two. I don't want to go to the toilet every thirty minutes while we're watching the film.

Maya Oh, film? What film?

Josh You're kidding, right? We wanted to go to the cinema tonight. Don't tell me you forgot!

Maya I'm so sorry, Josh, but I did forget. I'm really stressed out at the moment. All these future plans! I always thought -Thank you! – I always thought life after school would be like a holiday. And then what happens? Oh, sorry! You have to think of so many things and meet thousands of people just to plan your career. I really admire you and Greg.

Josh You admire me and Greg? I'm surprised!

Maya Greg has always known he wants to be a chef. So he's using his gap year to take a trip to Asia. He's living and breathing Asian cuisine. And he wants to study it right from scratch. He's in Thailand now, and then he wants to visit Cambodia, Vietnam, Laos. I think that's fantastic! Imagine all those different foods he'll be able to try out. And you, you've managed to get a placement at a big London newspaper, who are now even sending you on a project in Paris! What am I going to do? I still don't know.

Josh But I always thought you wanted to be an actress and go to drama school.

Maya I still do. But I talked to my parents about it and I think they're right: I should try something else while I'm applying to drama schools, just to be on the safe side. That way I could pick up some new skills and see if I'm good at other things, too.

Josh It's a good idea. And what will that be?

Maya Well, I don't know yet. But, to help me find out, I've got an appointment with a careers officer, who I'm meeting in ten minutes! Oh, why am I always late these days? Life is killing me! Bye, Josh!

Josh Bye! Always a drama! *To the girls sitting by the door.* Hi! What are you doing tonight?

Unit 2 Travelling for work

Grammar

1 ***Relative pronouns*. This is a logic puzzle. Read the instructions below and solve the puzzle.**

Five men of different nationalities* live in five houses next to each other in a street. Each house is a different colour. The five men – a Brit (a British person), an American, a German, a Norwegian and an Austrian – play different sports, like different drinks, and have different pets.

1 Below are some clues about the five men. Quickly complete the clues with *who*, *which* or *where*.
2 Use the clues to complete the table.
3 Now from the table write down the nationality of the man who has a fish as a pet.

a The house _where_ the Brit lives is red.

b The American has dogs as pets.

c The Austrian drinks tea.

d The green house is the house __________ is on the immediate left of the white house.

e The man __________ lives in green house drinks coffee.

f The man __________ plays tennis has birds as pets.

g The man __________ lives in the yellow house plays football.

h The man in the house in the middle drinks milk.

i The man __________ plays golf lives next door to the one __________ has cats.

j The man __________ keeps horses lives next door to the man __________ plays football.

k The man __________ plays squash drinks chocolate.

l The German plays basketball.

m The Norwegian lives next to the house __________ is blue.

n The man __________ plays golf has a neighbour __________ drinks water.

NATIONALITY	Norwegian	Austrian	Brit	German	American
HOUSE COLOUR					
DRINK					
SPORT					
PET					

The man who has a fish as a pet is the ______________________________

→ * nationality: *Staatsangehörigkeit*

Vocabulary

2 Travel crossword. First, finish the definitions with *who*, *which* or *where*, then write the words into the crossword. All the words are about travel.

Down

1 The form which you fill in when you arrive at a hotel is a … form.

2 A person _______ travels by plane, train etc. is a …

3 The place _______ people check your clothes and baggage at an airport is the … check.

5 The thing _______ opens the door of your hotel room.

6 The things _______ you carry when you travel.

8 The person _______ checks in people at an airport is a check-in …

10 The place _______ you go for your plane.

11 Someone _______ checks your bags when you arrive at an aiport is a … officer.

14 Someone _______ isn't a child and is over 18 is an …

Across

1 A man or woman _______ works at the reception desk in a hotel is a …

4 A small book _______ gives you information (e.g. about a hotel).

7 A man _______ works in business.

9 A room _______ is for one person.

12 The document _______ you get when you check in at an airport and _______ gives you your gate number is a … card.

13 Something _______ you need when you travel to another country.

15 The place _______ you check in at an airport is the check-in … and at a hotel it's the reception …

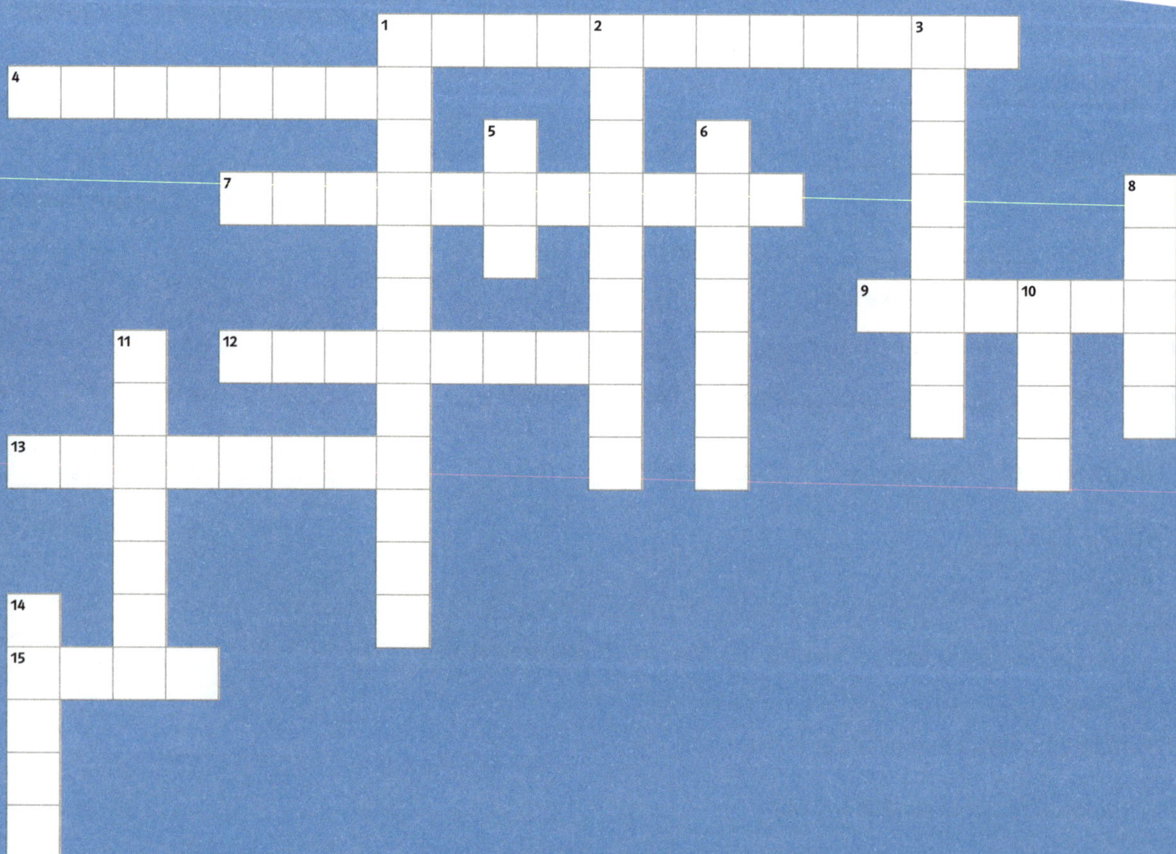

Writing

In the tasks which follow you are going to look at booking a hotel room for a businessman, Mr Rosenberg, who is going on a trip to Chicago.

3 Leonie Koch is a secretary in an American company in Germany called Star Communications. Next week, her boss Joe Rosenberg will be in the States. He is talking to Leonie about his trip. Read their conversation and complete Leonie's notes below.

Leonie When will you be in Chicago, Mr Rosenberg?
Joe On Wednesday and Thursday next week.
Leonie That's October 17 and 18.
Joe Right. My first meeting on Wednesday is at 9.30, so I'll need a hotel for the night before, Tuesday night.
Leonie And when will you leave Chicago?
Joe My last meeting there finishes at midday on Thursday. Then I'll fly back.
Leonie So you don't want to stay overnight on Thursday?
Joe No, I have too much to do here!
Leonie And about the hotel. You just want a single room, of course. Anything else special?
Joe The hotel should be near the city centre, if possible. Oh, and one with a swimming pool would be great.
Leonie Fine. I'll make the arrangements.

Hotel arrangements for
Mr Rosenberg's trip to Chicago:
Room: single room
Number of nights: ______
Dates: ______

Special notes about the hotel:
Where? ______
Other: ______

4 Finding a hotel. Leonie looked on the Internet for hotels for Mr Rosenberg. Here are two. Which one is better? Why? Write one or two sentences below.

O'Hare Inn, Chicago ★★★★

Rooms	325
Location	O'Hare International Airport, Chicago. Only 2 minutes from the airport terminal. Ideal for business travelers.
Facilities	Restaurant, bar, fitness center, parking, Internet access, 4 conference centers

Belmont Hotel, Chicago ★★★★

Rooms	214 all smoke free
Location	Downtown Chicago. One block from the John Hancock Center, Water Tower and Magnificent Mile shopping
Facilities	Restaurant, bar, sauna, swimming pool, fitness center, parking, roof garden, Internet access

I think the best hotel is ______________ because ______________

____

5 Next, Leonie phones the hotel in Chicago. Complete the conversation with the information you have already and suitable words.

Receptionist Belmont, Chicago. Anita speaking. How may I help you this morning?

Leonie Good morning. I'd like to book a room, please.

Receptionist Certainly. Could you give me the dates, please?

Leonie It's for two nights from **(1)** ______________

Receptionist And is that a single or a double room?

Leonie **(2)** ______________

Receptionist Smoking or non-smoking?

Leonie **(3)** ______________

Receptionist Yes, that looks fine. Can I take your name?

Leonie The room is for **(4)** ______________, that's R- **(5)** ______________, from **(6)** ______________ in Germany.

Receptionist Will Mr Rosenberg pay for the room personally?

Leonie No, the company will pay.

Receptionist Thank you. That's all booked. Could you send me a fax to confirm the booking?

Leonie Sure, I'll do that straight away.

Receptionist Thank you. And thank you for choosing the Belmont Hotel.

6 Leonie sends the fax below. Complete it with the correct phrases.

Leonie Koch, Star Communications GmbH & Co, Germany — Please note that — Dates: — Reservations, Belmont Hotel, Chicago, IL — Room: — made today by telephone for — Confirmation of telephone reservation

FAX

Star Communications GmbH & Co
121 Hofstraße
06886 Wittenberg
Germany
Fax: +49-3491-6200

To:	(1) ________
Fax Number:	001-773-488-3030
Date:	20….-September-23
Subject:	(2) ________
From:	(3) ________

This is to confirm the room reservation **(4)** ________ Mr J. Rosenberg from our company:

(5) ________ Two nights, October 16 and 17 **(6)** ________ Single room

(7) ________ Star Communications will pay Mr Rosenberg's bill directly and in full.

Leonie Koch

Video lounge

7 The video contains some useful words that you can learn about jobs and choosing a career. Watch part 1 of the video again.

1. First, use your dictionary to write in the German translations of the words and phrases below.
2. Watch the video and tick (✓) the words when you hear them.
3. Choose two words or phrases and write a sentence with each on a separate sheet of paper.

	English	German	✓
a	questionnaire	Fragebogen	☐
b	to make a living (doing sth.)	________	☐
c	good job prospects	________	☐
d	to suit (your abilities and interests)	________	☐
e	to belong to (a club)	________	☐
f	(your) strengths	________	☐
g	to deal with (people)	________	☐
h	alphabetical (job list)	________	☐
i	job description	________	☐
j	one of the main duties of a …	________	☐

Unit 3 Apprenticeships

Grammar

1 Read about these three jobs from around the world.

1

Country: Canada
Job: mountain rescue worker
In western Canada, there are some high mountains. They're called the Rocky Mountains (or 'the Rockies'). Mountain rescue workers rescue people in the mountains. The job can be hard and dangerous.

2

Country: USA
Job: deli assistant
New York is famous for its delis (delicatessens) where you can buy deli sandwiches and bagels. Deli assistants make sandwiches and serve customers. There are always lots of customers and the assistants work very quickly!

3

Country: Australia
Job: road train driver
Road trains are monster lorries 50 metres long. They have over 60 wheels and they travel at 100 kph. Road train drivers travel all over Australia. They're often on the road for days and they sleep at night in their lorries. The job can be lonely!

2 Finish the sentences about the jobs. All the sentences are *if-sentences type 2*.

1 If you had the job in text 1, you would be in ____________________ (country?).

2 If you __________________ (have) the job in text 2, you __________________ (be) in New York.

3 You _______________ (be) in _______________ (country?) if you _______________ (have) the job in text 3.

4 If you were a mountain rescue worker, you ____________________ (do what?).

5 You _______________ (make) sandwiches if you _______________ (be) a deli assistant.

6 If you _______________ (be) a road train driver, you ________________________________ (do what?).

→ * mountain rescue: *Bergwacht* → ** to rescue: *retten* → *** wheel: *Rad* → **** lonely: *einsam*

3 **Look back at exercise 1 again on the last page. Answer these questions in full sentences. Use *if-sentences type 2* again.**

1 What mountains would you work in if you were a mountain rescue worker in Canada?

If I was a mountain rescue worker in Canada, I would work in the ____________________

2 How would you work if you worked in a deli in New York? (quickly? slowly?)

If ____________________

3 Where would you sleep at night if you drove a road train in Australia?

If ____________________

Vocabulary

4 **Job ads. Below are some expressions which you often find in job advertisements. Use them to complete the two ads.**

WANTED

MECHANIC **(1)** to work in our busy car repair workshop. Applicants must be **(2)** ____________.

For further **(3)** ____________, please **(4)** ____________ Martin Reynolds on **(0212)** 743-744.

part time | Hours | experience | contact | information | fully qualified | skills | careers@techno...com | to work | looking for

We are **(5)** ____________ a

SECRETARY

to work **(6)** ____________ in our office.

(7) ____________:

Mon–Thurs. 9 a.m. – 1 p.m.

Applicants must have good computer **(8)** ____________ and have **(9)** ____________ in office work.

Interested? Please email us at:

(10) ____________

5 **CVs. Here are some expressions which you often find on CVs. Match the English expressions and their German translations.**

1 personal details	a Geburtsdatum
2 date of birth	b Ausbildung
3 education	c Hobbies / Interessen
4 qualifications	d Persönliche Daten / Angaben zur Person
5 primary school	e Grundschule
6 secondary school	f Qualifikationen / Abschlüsse
7 work experience	g weiterführende Schule
8 skills	h Kenntnisse, Fähigkeiten
9 interests	i Berufserfahrung

6 **Do the crossword. All the words were in the unit.**

Across

1 Handwerker *pl.*
5 *erfahren, sachkundig*
8 It's a great … to practise your English. *Gelegenheit, Möglichkeit*
10 Freizeit (2 words)
11 The job you get depends partly on your … *Begabung, Können*
12 My English is …. *fließend*
14 A flight … works on a plane.
17 The exam which English pupils take at age 16. (4 letters)

Down

2 another way to say 'immediately' *gleich, sofort* (2 words)
3 My favourite … is maths. *Fach*
4 You … a job, apprenticeship etc. *sich um etw bewerben* (2 words)
6 We are … looking for trainees. *momentan, zurzeit*
7 Can you give me some …, please? *Rat*
9 another word for apprenticeship (T…)
13 mother … *(Mutter) sprache*
15 You … or do an exam. *machen, ablegen*
16 Apprentices earn a basic …. *Lohn*

Writing

7 **Write your CV. Begin as below. Write on a separate piece of paper.**

CURRICULUM VITAE

PERSONAL DETAILS

Name: ______________________

Address: ______________________

Date of birth: ______________________

EDUCATION AND QUALIFICATIONS

8 **Writing a letter of application. When Meryem Gulec contacted Air Deutschland about a traineeship (in your book on page 60), she sent her CV and wrote a covering letter. You can see her letter below. Look at the letter and read the notes on the next page.**

1 Findorffstraße 20
28215 Bremen

2 Mr H. Werner
Personnel Manager
Air Deutschland
Schönefelder Straße 100
12521 Berlin

3 3 March 20…

4 Dear Mr Werner

5 **Traineeship**

6 I am writing to apply for one of the traineeships which you advertised in last week's edition of International Flight Magazine. I am interested in a traineeship as a flight attendant.

I am currently a full-time student at a vocational college in Bremen. I will complete my course in summer next year and hope to get a qualification as a Management Assistant for Travel and Tourism (Kauffrau für Touristik und Freizeit). I enclose my CV.

For the last year I have had a part-time job at Hapag-Lloyd travel agents in Bremen. I am keen to learn, work hard, and my English is good. I would very much welcome the opportunity to work for you as a trainee.

I look forward to hearing from you soon.

7 Yours sincerely

Meryem Gulec

8 Meryem Gulec (Ms)

9 Enc.

→ * to advertise: *ausschreiben* → ** to complete: *abschließen* → *** to enclose: *beilegen* → **** keen to learn: *lernbegierig*

WRITING A FORMAL PERSONAL LETTER

1 Your address. In Britain and the USA you *do not* write your name here.
2 The inside address (the person, company etc.) you are writing to.
3 Date. Always write the date in words – if you use numbers it can be confusing. In the UK 04.06.20.. is 4 June (as in Germany) but in the U.S. it would be 6 April.
4 The salutation.
5 The subject. Use bold letters or underline the subject so that it stands out.
6 The body of the letter. Remember that in English this always begins with a CAPITAL LETTER.
7 The close. The most usual close for all professional correspondence is *Yours sincerely*.
8 Sign your name and then type it again below your signature.
9 *Enc.* is short for *enclosure(s)*. It means you have put in (enclosed) another document with your letter (here a CV).

9 Now YOU. You see this advertisement on a website called *Lehrstellen...de* for apprenticeships with a large German pharmaceuticals company. Write a letter of application. Write on a separate sheet of paper.

LAROCHE PHARMA DEUTSCHLAND currently has apprenticehips for laboratory technicians, marketing assistants and office administrative assistants. If you are interested in training with one of the world's top companies, write to Ms J. Bridges, Rheinstraße 2-4, 60316 Frankfurt am Main, enclosing your CV.

Video lounge

10 Watching films and videos is a good way to learn new words and phrases which you can use in everyday conversation. Watch the video and try to find the English expressions for the German ones below. Tip: the expressions are in the right order – you will hear number 1 first, then number 2, and so on.

1 Flippe nicht aus (bleib gelassen) ______
2 (am Telefon) Hallo, (Name) am Apparat ______
3 Bis dann! ______
4 (jemand klopft an die Tür) Herein! ______
5 Nehmen Sie bitte Platz ______
6 Praktikum ______
7 Gut. Weiter ______
8 klingt gut! ______
9 als erstes ______
10 rund um die Uhr ______
11 sonst noch etwas? ______
12 ganz gleich, was passiert ______
13 eine Möglichkeit wäre... ______
14 normaleweise ______
15 Ich habe es nicht so gemeint ______
16 natürlich nicht ______
17 Gratuliere! ______

Unit 4 A visit to a company

Grammar

1 **Write in the forms of the English *adverbs* and the German word which translates both the *adjective* and the *adverb*.**

	Adjective	Adverb	Deutsch
Die meisten Adverbien werden gebildet, indem *-ly* an das Adjectiv gehängt wird. Das gilt auch für Adjective, die in *-l* und *-e* (außer *-le*) enden.			
1	bad	badly	schlecht
2	careful		
3	exact		
4	quick		
5	quiet		
6	slow		
7	urgent		
8	(inter)national		
9	central		
10	local		
11	punctual		
12	(un)usual		
13	polite		
Bei Adjektiven mit der Endung *-y* wird *-y* zu *-ily*.			
14	angry		
15	easy		
16	happy		
17	healthy		
18	hungry		
19	noisy		
Die Endung *-le* wird zu *-ly*.			
20	fashionable		
21	reasonable		
22	simple		
23	terrible		
-ic wird zu *-ically*.			
24	automatic		
25	basic		
26	dramatic		
Das Adverb von *good* ist *well*.			
27	good		

2 **In the pairs of sentences below, one sentence needs an *adjective* and the other an *adverb*. Complete the sentences with the correct forms. All the words were in your table on page 14.**

1 **punctual**
   a My boss is a very _punctual_ person.
   b She always arrives _punctually_ for meetings.

2 **healthy**
   a It's important to have a ______ diet.
   b You should eat ______ .

3 **international**
   a The company operates ______ .
   b It is an ______ company.

4 **good**
   a They speak English ______ .
   b Their knowledge of English is very ______ .

5 **quiet**
   a He has a ______ voice.
   b He speaks ______ .

6 **fashionable**
   a She always dresses ______ .
   b She wears ______ clothes.

7 **local**
   a It is good to buy as many things as you can ______ .
   b Use ______ shops and services whenever you can.

8 **simple**
   a Can you give me a ______ explanation?
   b Can you explain that ______ ?

Tom sometimes reacts angrily to phone calls.

3 **Complete these sentences with a suitable *adjective* or *adverb* from your table on page 14.**

1 Is it an _automatic_ process?
Yes, computers and robots do everything in the factory.
2 That machine is dangerous. Use it ______ .
3 Could you send us a ______ answer to this email? We need the information immediately.
4 It is important to speak to people ______ – say 'please' and 'thank you' often, for example.
5 This is an ______ diagram of the building. All the details are there and they are 100 % accurate.
6 This exercise is not difficult at all – I can do it ______ .
7 My English isn't very good. Could you speak ______ and clearly for me, please?
8 His last meal had been yesterday and he ate the food ______ .

Vocabulary

4 Factory vocabulary. First write in the German translations of the expressions below, then use some of the words and phrases from the table to complete the text.

1 area (of a factory)	______	10 quality control	______
2 dispatch	______	11 raw materials	______
3 entrance	______	12 research and development	______
4 laboratory	______	13 to invent	______
5 lorry	______	14 to load	______
6 offices	______	15 to store	______
7 process	______	16 warehouse	______
8 product	______		
9 production	______		

WELCOME TO SUNTECH

Want to visit our factory? There are weekly guided tours of our factory. For more information please contact Debbie Harris on 0800 548319 or email us at tours@suntech.co…uk.

SunTech is one of Europe's leading manufacturers of solar panels*.

How our factory works

The process begins in our laboratory, in our **(1)** research and development department**. This is where we **(2)** ______ new products. Next, we make the products and for that we need to buy the **(3)** ______ which we use to make the panels. We buy these and we **(4)** ______ them in the factory until we need them. We make the panels in the **(5)** ______ area of the factory. Lots of the processes here are computer controlled and very technically advanced. After manufacture, we store the panels again in our **(6)** ______ but first we have to test them for quality and that happens in the **(7)** ______ department. Now, the products are ready to sell. This is where the people in our **(8)** ______ are important. These are the employees who market and sell the products. They take orders*** for the panels. When a customer orders panels, the dispatch department **(9)** ______ the products onto lorries which deliver the panels to the customers.

→ * solar panel: *Solarkollektor* ** department: *Abteilung* *** order: *Bestellung*

5 **Do the crossword. All the words were in the unit.**

Down

1 After our visit we wrote a …. *Bericht*
2 *Hersteller*
3 Abbreviation for Do It Yourself. *Heimwerken*
4 … to meet you.
5 *nebenbei bemerkt* (3 words)
9 *TechnikerIn*
10 Our … is in London. *Hauptsitz* (2 words)
14 When all goes well, firms can … quickly. *wachsen*
15 The company makes lots of different … of products. *Arten*

Across

6 I have an … with Mrs Watson at 10 o'clock. *Termin*
7 Can I … my assistant? *vorstellen*
8 The place where you go into a building. *Eingang*
11 *Azubi, Lehrling*
12 Please come …. *hier entlang* (2 words)
13 … that you could work in England. *Stell dir vor*
16 Let me show you … our offices.

Writing

6 **Imagine that you are one of the apprentices in Unit 3 in your book and that you have a good friend who is English-speaking. Write your friend an email. Say you are in England this week, what you did today (visit Rolac), where you are staying, and give your impressions of England, the weather, the food etc. Begin like this and continue on a separate sheet of paper.**

Hi ____________________ *(name)*

This week I'm in England! I'm here with… ______________________________

____

____

____

____

Video lounge

7 Below is Maya's telephone conversation with the Chinese businessman, Mr Cheng Xiao. Watch and write in the missing words and phrases, then act out the conversation with a partner.

A second telephone rings. Maya picks it up.

Maya *Ryam Hotel. Sie sprechen mit Maya Conway. Was kann ich für Sie tun?*

Mr Xiao My name is Xiao Cheng. I would like to make a reservation.

Maya Certainly, sir. Just one moment please. *To Miss Schmidt.* Someone wants to make a reservation.

Miss Schmidt When?

Maya *On the phone.* When would you like **(1)** ______________, please?

Mr Xiao I'd like to stay for five nights from the **(2)** ______________.

Maya Five nights, from the **(3)** ______________.

Mr Xiao No, from the **(4)** ______________.

Maya Oh, sorry, from the **(5)** ______________.

Mr Xiao OK, yeah. Five nights.

Maya Yes, we do have a room free then, sir. Could you spell your name for me, please?

Mr Xiao Certainly. It's X-I-A-O and C-H-E-N-G.

Maya Thank you, Mr **(6)** ______________.

Mr Xiao No, it's Mr **(7)** ______________. In Chinese the family name is placed before the given name.

Maya Oh, I didn't know that, Mr Xiao. Very interesting, though, thank you. Would you like a **(8)** ______________?

Mr Xiao A single, please. A non-smoker.

Maya That's absolutely fine, Mr Xiao.

Mr Xiao Thank you. Bye.

Maya Bye.

Unit 5 Global business

Grammar

1 **The *simple present passive*. Read the text about how a typical British supermarket works, then finish the sentences below. Use the *simple present passive*.**

How a supermarket in the UK gets and sells its goods

First, the supermarket company's 'buyers' buy the goods. They buy some goods in the UK, but they buy a lot of things – like wine, and oranges and other fruit – in countries around the world.

Next, the supermarket company stores the goods. It stores them in big warehouses called 'distribution centres'. The company has distribution centres around the UK.

After that lorries transport the goods from the distribution centres to the different supermarkets. The lorries often deliver the goods at night, so that they are on sale fresh in the morning.

Finally, customers buy the goods at the supermarkets. At the checkouts, the checkout assistants put the barcodes of the goods into a computer. The company uses this information to order more goods.

First, the goods **(1)** __are bought__ (buy) by the company's buyers. Some goods **(2)** ____________ (buy) in the UK, but other goods **(3)** ____________ (buy) in countries around the world. Next the goods **(4)** ____________ (store) in big warehouses called distribution centres. After that the goods **(5)** ____________ (transport) by lorries to the company's supermarkets. The goods **(6)** ____________ often ____________ (deliver) at night. Finally, the goods **(7)** ____________ (buy) by customers. The barcodes **(8)** ____________ (put) into a computer by the checkout assistants. This information **(9)** ____________ (use) by the supermarket to order more goods.

→ * distribution centre: *Vertriebszentrum* ** checkout: *Kasse* *** barcode: *Strichkode*

2 **The *simple past passive*. Do this quiz about the history of some everyday products. (Answers at the bottom of page 26.)**

1 popcorn	**2** aspirins	**3** paper	**4** chocolate
	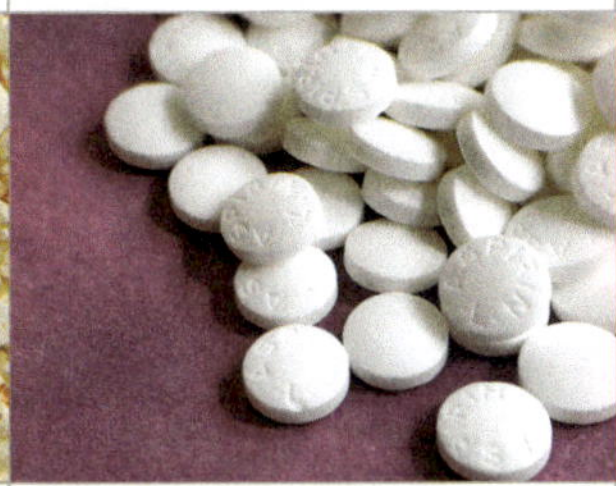		
Everyone likes popcorn at the cinema. But who invented it? **a** Alfred T. Popcorn **b** Native Americans **c** Walt Disney	People use aspirins every day. But who invented them? **a** a German scientist **b** Mary-Ann Aspirin **c** an English scientist	Paper is 5,000 years old. But where was the first paper made? **a** in India **b** in France **c** in Egypt	When and where was chocolate discovered? **a** in 1500 in Europe **b** about 2,000 years ago in Mexico **c** 4,000 years ago in China
I think that popcorn was invented by ____________ ____________ ____________	I think that aspirins were ____________ ____________ ____________	I think that the first paper ____________ ____________ ____________	Chocolate ____________ ____________ ____________ ____________

3 **Translate into English. All the sentences are *passive*.**

1 Dieses Bier wird in Deutschland produziert.

This beer is produced in Germany.

2 Diese Computerbildschirme werden in Japan hergestellt.

____

3 Mein neuer Computer wurde gestern geliefert.

____

4 Unsere Produkte werden weltweit verkauft.

____

5 Englisch wird in vielen Ländern gesprochen.

____

6 Viele neue Gebäude wurden in den Sechzigerjahren gebaut.

____

7 Unsere Produkte werden nicht in den USA verkauft.

____

8 Der Junge wurde nur ein Euro für seine Arbeit bezahlt (*to pay sb.*).

____

Vocabulary

4 Do the crossword. All the words were in the unit.

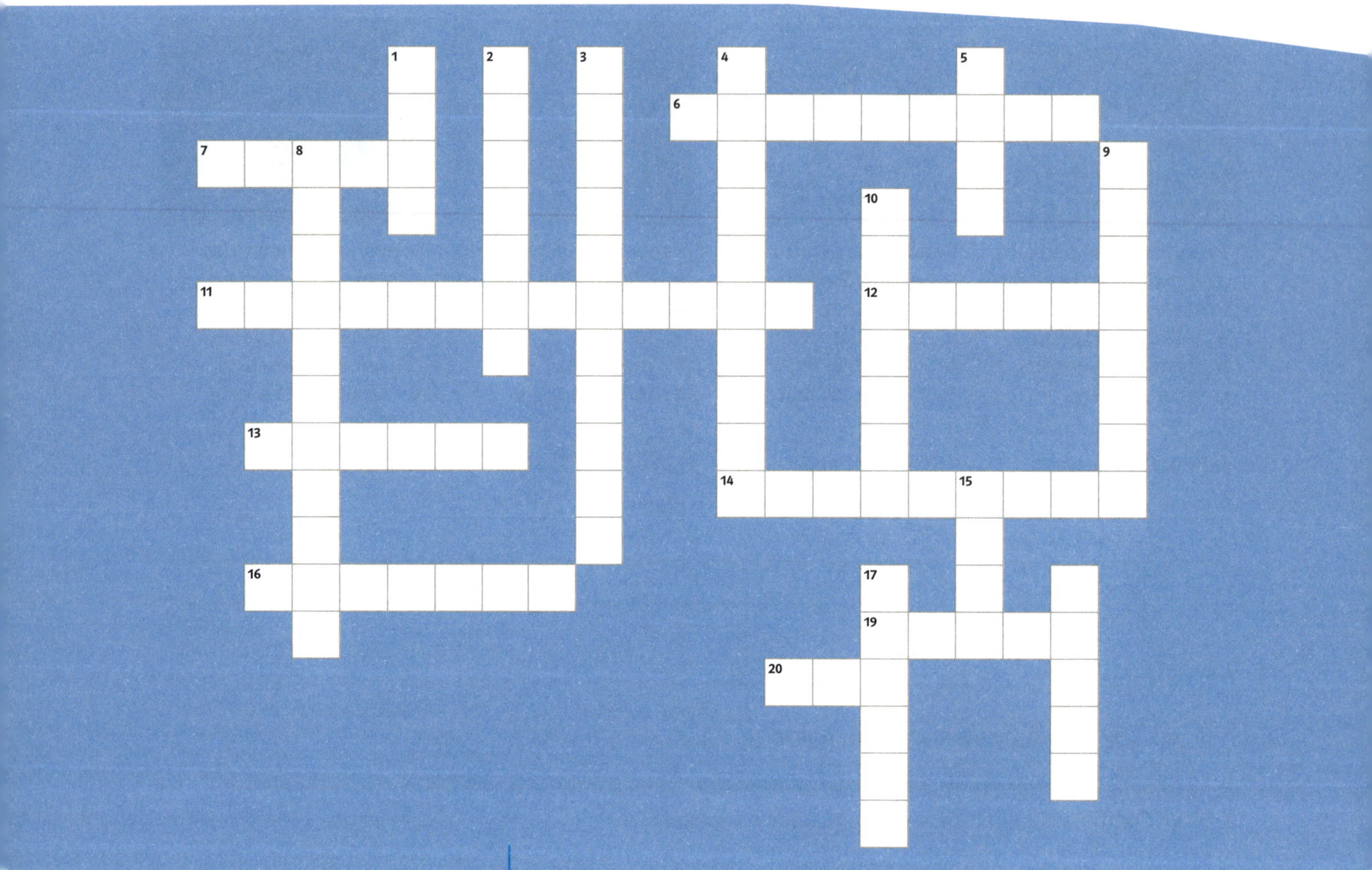

Down

1 He doesn't ... much money. *verdienen*
2 You can phone this when you need help. *Telefonauskunftsstelle, Hotline*
3 to ... *herstellen*
4 Many people in India work in a .... There are lots of telephones here. (2 words)
5 *Bergwerk*
8 The company sells its products on the ... *Weltmarkt* (2 words)
9 We ... the computers in Ireland. *zusammenstellen*
10 to ... *produzieren*
15 past participle of the verb *to sell*
17 past participle of the verb *to buy*
18 past participle of the verb *to grow*

Across

6 Every computer has a .... *Festplatte* (2 words)
7 Some desktop computers have a .... *Computer-Turm*
11 a place in California (around San Francisco) where there are many hi-tech companies (2 words)
12 Goods from around the world are ... in this shop. *zum Verkauf (stehen)* (2 words)
13 a place where bread is made
14 the opposite of cheap
16 to ...: *liefern*
19 to ...: *bestellen*
20 abbreviation for central processing unit *Hauptprozessor*

Answers Unit 4 exercise 2

1 b Native Americans
2 a a German scientist
3 c in Egypt
4 b about 2,000 years ago in Mexico

Writing

5 The *passive* is often used to describe processes. We also often use words like *first*, *then*, *next* when we describe a process. Below you can see a diagram which shows how tomato ketchup is made.

A Here are some words you will need to describe the process of manufacturing ketchup. Match the English and German expressions. Use your dictionary if necessary.

1 to harvest	a etw. (bei einer Temperatur von ... Grad) behalten
2 to transport	b entfernen
3 to chop	c ernten
4 to pre-cook	d Gewürze
5 to pulp	e hinzugeben
6 to remove	f in Flaschen füllen
7 skin (of a tomato)	g kleinhacken
8 seeds (of a tomato)	h Samen
9 to add	i Schale
10 spices	j transportieren
11 to keep sth. (at a temperature of ... degrees)	k vorkochen
12 to bottle	l zermalmen

B Now look at the diagram. The notes will help you to understand it.

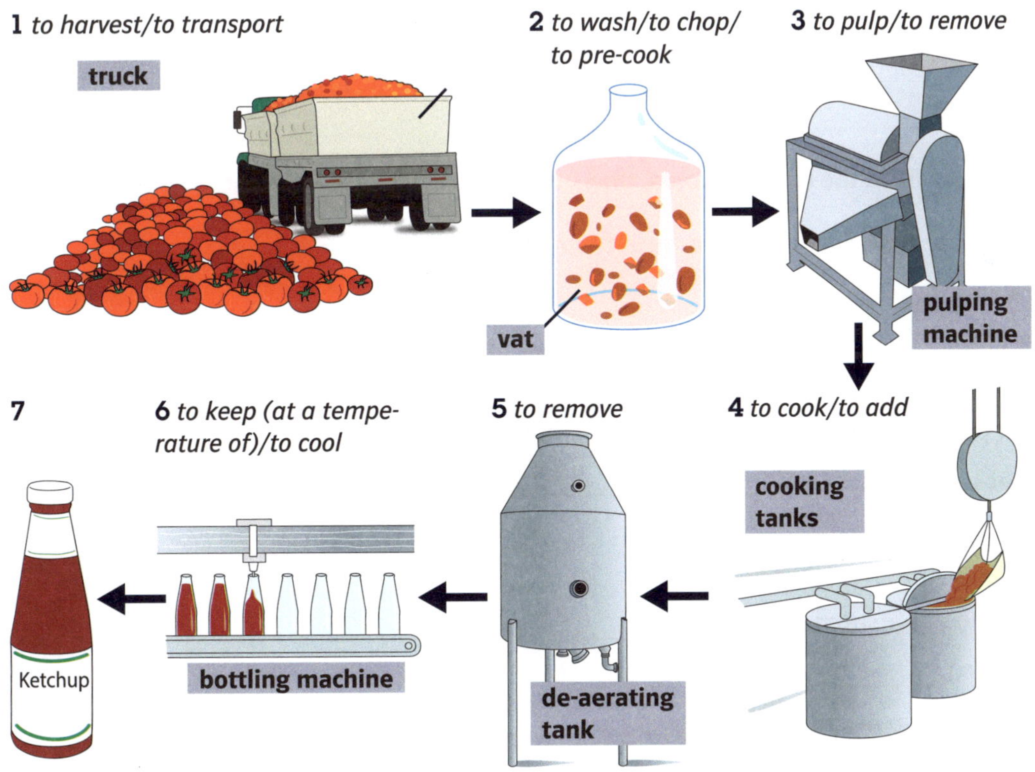

1 Farmers grow the tomatoes and trucks transport them to the factory.
2 In the factory, they wash, chop and pre-cook the tomatoes in big metal vats.
3 Pulping machines pulp the tomatoes and remove the skins and seeds.
4 They cook the tomatoes in big cooking tanks and add spices.
5 It is necessary to remove the air in the ketchup. De-aerating tanks do this.
6 They keep the ketchup at a temperature of 90°C while they bottle it. This kills any bacteria.
7 And now you have ketchup!

C Now YOU. Write a description of the manufacturing process for tomato ketchup. Use the simple present *passive* and the words on the right. Begin like this:

First, the tomatoes are harvested and they are transported to the factory by trucks. Only the very best quality tomatoes are used to manufacture ketchup. In the factory ______

First, …
Then …
Next, …
After that, …
Finally, …

Video lounge

6 **Watch the video and fill in the missing words, then act out the conversation with a partner.**

Maya *To man at desk.* Einen Moment, bitte. *She rings Mr Xiao.*

Mr Xiao Hello.

Maya Mr Xiao? It's Maya Conway **(1)** ______ from the Ryam Hotel.

Mr Xiao Oh, OK.

Maya I'm so sorry, sir, but I forgot to ask for your **(2)** ______ details. Could you please give me the **(3)** ______ and tell me when it's valid* to?

Mr Xiao Certainly.

Maya Thank you.

Mr Xiao It's a MasterCard. The number is **(4)** ______ and it's valid until **(5)** ______.

Maya Thank you so much, Mr Xiao. **(6)** ______ welcoming you here on the twenty-fourth.

Mr Xiao Thank you. Goodbye.

Maya Bye. Oh!

→ * valid: *gültig*

Unit 6 A month in New Zealand

Grammar

1 The *present perfect* with *since* and *for*. Read the '*Since* oder *for?*' box and look at these time expressions. Which describe a 'point in time' *(Zeitpunkt)* and which describe a 'period of time' *(Zeitraum)*? Complete the two lists.

ten years · last Monday · the beginning of June · I was small · 2010 · 8 o'clock · a (very) long time! · 20 minutes · 23 January · yesterday · I started at college · four hours · three months · six days · two weeks · ages*

Point in time *(Zeitpunkt)*		Period of time *(Zeitraum)*	
1	8 o'clock	a	ten years
2		b	
3		c	
4		d	
5		e	
6		f	
7		g	
8		h	

Since oder *for*?

Im Deutschen benutzt man das Wort *seit*, um darüber zu sprechen, wie lange man schon etwas macht:
Ich bin seit acht Uhr in der Schule.
Ich wohne (schon) seit zehn Jahren hier.
Im Englischen braucht man für diese beiden Sätze zwei unterschiedliche Wörter.
*I have been at school **since** 8 o'clock.*
*I have lived here **for** ten years.*
Im Englischen kommt es also darauf an, ob man über einen Zeitpunkt *(since)* oder einen Zeitraum *(for)* spricht. Im ersten Satz sagt der Sprecher, dass er seit einem bestimmten Zeitpunkt (8 Uhr) in der Schule ist. Im zweiten Satz nennt der Sprecher den Zeitraum, in dem er schon hier wohnt (10 Jahre).

2 Use expressions from exercise 1 to complete these sentences. There is often more than one answer.

1 Nicole has lived in the town where she lives now for 10 years.
2 I'm in the doctor's waiting room at the moment. I've been here ______.
3 Three months ago we moved to a new flat. I've lived here now ______.
4 I've loved gymnastics ______.
5 It feels like this English lesson has lasted ______.
6 I've known my best friend ______.
7 I've had a really bad headache** ______.

→ * ages: *eine Ewigkeit* → ** a headache: *Kopfschmerzen*

3 ***Present perfect*** **or** ***simple past*****? Complete this text with the correct forms.**

Martine Young is 19 and she lives in New Zealand. Her dad, Rod, is a sheep farmer on the South Island. Her mum, Sheila, is a teacher at the local secondary school. Sheep are an important industry in New Zealand. In fact, for every one person in the country there are 12 sheep! This is the story of Martine and her family.

The story begins with Rod's grandparents – Martine's great grandparents*. They **(1)** came ____________ (to come) to New Zealand from Scotland in 1933. Grandpa and Grandma Young **(2)** ____________ (to work) hard in their new homecountry and in 1938 they **(3)** ____________ (to buy) a farm. It is the same farm that Martine and her parents live on today, so the family **(4)** ____________ (to be) on the farm for almost 80 years.
In the early years of the farm, back in the 1940s and 50s, the Youngs **(5)** ____________ (to have) different sorts of animals and they also **(6)** ____________ (to grow) wheat**. But when Martine's dad **(7)** ____________ (to take over) the farm, he **(8)** ____________ (to decide) to concentrate on sheep. He **(9)** ____________ (to produce) lamb*** and wool now for over forty years. Much of the meat is exported to Britain.
Martine loves life on the farm and since she was small, she **(10)** ____________ (to help) her dad with the sheep. She has no brothers or sisters and one day, she wants to take over the farm from her dad.
Martine **(11)** ____________ (to leave) school last year and since last summer she **(12)** ____________ (to be) a student at an agricultural college**** in Christchurch where she is learning about all the modern techniques of sheep farming. She will become the next generation of Youngs to work on the family farm.

→ * great grandparents: *Urgroßeltern* → **wheat: *Weizen* → *** lamb: *Lammfleisch* → **** agricultural college: *Landwirtschaftsschule*

Vocabulary

4 The departments of a company. Write the names of the departments into the diagram, then complete the table with the German translations. Use your dictionary if necessary.

RESEARCH & DEVELOPMENT (R&D) SALES DISTRIBUTION (LOGISTICS) ACCOUNTS QUALITY CONTROL PRODUCTION PURCHASING HUMAN RESOURCES (HR) MARKETING

1 R&D 'We develop new products here in the company's laboratory.'	2 ____ 'We buy the raw materials we need to make our products.'	3 ____ 'We make the products here in the company's factory.'
4 ____ 'We test the products for quality before they leave the factory.'	5 ____ 'We advertise (promote) the products.'	6 ____ 'We sell the products.'
7 ____ 'We distribute* the products.'	8 ____ 'We look after the company's finances**.'	9 ____ 'We recruit*** and train new employees and look after them when they are

Research & development	Forschung und Entwicklung	Marketing	____
Accounts	____	Production	____
Distribution	____	Purchasing	____
Human resources	____	Quality control	____
		Sales	____

5 Many job titles in English end in *-er* just like in German. But not all! Finish the job titles below.

1 farm er	6 electric____	11 supervis____****
2 hairdress____	7 technic____	12 auth____
3 office work____	8 engin____	13 scient____
4 manag____	9 doct____	14 psycholog____
5 mechan____	10 film direct____	15 therap____

→ * to distribute: *vertreiben* → ** finances: *Finanzen* → *** to recruit: *einstellen* → **** *Aufsichtsperson, Dienstvorgesetzte(r)*

Writing

6 Some New Zealand teenagers are at a beach party. Look at what they're saying (A – E) and write some suitable answers.

A ______

B ______

C ______

D ______

E ______

7 You are in an English-speaking country. How could you say these things?

1 Verzeihung. Könnten Sie mir bitte helfen?

______

2 Wie geht's euch heute Morgen?

______

3 (Would you like some more pancakes?) Ja bitte. Sie sind lecker!

______

8 **Using *Could you* to write polite sentences. In emails and letters at work, it is more polite for English speakers to write sentences with *Could you (please)* than to say things more directly. Rewrite the sentences below using *Could you*.**

1 Send us your new catalogue.

Could you please send us your new catalogue?

2 Let us know when you will arrive at the airport.

3 Tell me the name of that nice hotel near the railway station.

4 Let me have your report next week.

Video lounge

9 **You learned in this unit how to be polite in English-speaking countries – and most people there are very polite. However, Florence in the video is very *impolite*!**

1 Watch the video and read the script of the first scene below. Underline the places where you think that Florence is impolite.
2 Write the scene again – try to make Florence more polite and friendly.
3 Act out your scene with a partner or in a small group.

Berlin, hotel reception

Maya Hi! Welcome to the Ryam Hotel! How can I help you?
Florence Hi! I'm Florence.
Maya Nice to meet you, Florence. Do you have a reservation?
Florence Sure! That's why I'm here, honey!
Maya Is Florence your family name?
Florence Are you kidding? You don't know who I am?
Maya No. No, sorry! I don't.
Florence I'm Florence Ryam. My grandad owns this place.
Nicole Hello, Ms Ryam! How are you?
Florence Hi! Fine, thanks. I just came from home – that's Texas – to promote my new perfume here in Berlin.
Maya Yes, Ms Ryam. We have reserved the Ambassador Suite for you. Here's your room key. Our porter will be more than happy to take up all your luggage for you. Oh, Ms Ryam? Breakfast is served from 6 until 10 o'clock on the first floor.
Florence I usually have breakfast at 12. Why do you serve breakfast down here?
Maya Down here? No, it's one floor above us.
Florence You mean the 2nd floor.
Maya Second? Oh, Americans call the ground floor the first floor, don't they?
Florence Yeah, right. Whatever. Porter? Come on!
Maya Enjoy your stay with us!

Unit 7 My job is special

Grammar

1 **The *past perfect*. Twenty years ago, the two men below began making and selling ice cream. They are now known around the world. Read their timeline and look at the sentences below. In each sentence, underline the action which came first.**

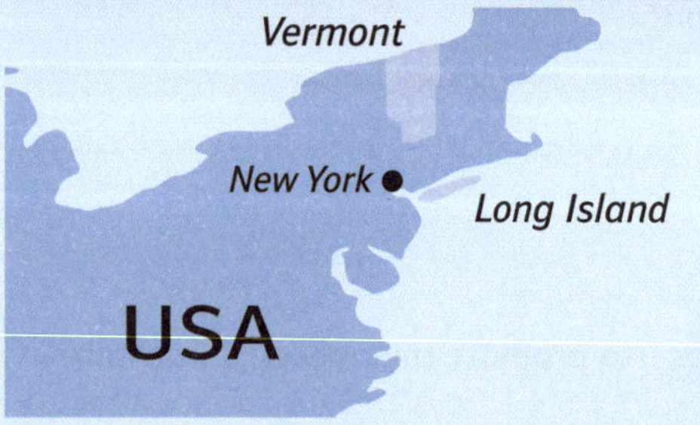

Timeline	
1993	Bill Greenfield and Perry Cohen met at high school on Long Island, New York. They soon became friends.
1997	The two men finished high school and went to live in Vermont.
1998	They decided to start a business together and went to college to learn how to make ice cream.
1999	They opened a small ice cream shop in their town. The ice cream became extremely popular.
2005	Bill and Perry opened an ice cream factory in a town two miles away.
2007	They started selling ice cream all over the USA.
2010	They opened factories and started selling ice cream first in Canada, then the UK, then Japan, and finally all over Europe.

EXAMPLE: Bill and Perry became friends after they had met at high school.

1 After they had finished high school, they both went to live in Vermont.
2 When they decided to start a business, they had already gone to live in Vermont.
3 They went to college to learn how to make ice cream because they had decided to start an ice cream business.
4 After they had learned how to make ice cream, they opened an ice cream shop in their town.

Das *past perfect*

Das *past perfect* wird in Sätzen oft zusammen mit dem *simple past* verwendet, um auszudrücken, dass ein Ereignis in der Vergangenheit vor einem anderen Ereignis geschehen ist. Diese Sätze enthalten oft Wörter wie *after*, *already*, *when* und *because*.
*When Mike **arrived*** (simple past) *at the station, the train **had** (already) **left*** (past perfect).

2 Look at Bill and Perry's timeline on page 34 and complete these sentences with the correct forms of the verbs – *simple past* or *past perfect*.

1 Two or three months after Bill and Perry ____________ (to open) their ice cream shop, their ice cream ____________ (to become) very popular in their town.

2 They ____________ (to open) their factory because their ice cream ____________ (to become) so popular.

3 Their ice cream ____________ (already/to become) popular in their town when they ____________ (to open) their factory.

4 After their ice cream ____________ (to become) so popular in their town, Bill and Perry ____________ (to decide) to sell it all over the USA.

5 They ____________ (to start) to sell their ice cream in other countries after it ____________ (to be) so popular in the USA.

6 They ____________ (can) sell ice cream in Canada because they ____________ (to build) a factory there.

7 When they ____________ (to start) to sell ice cream in Britain, they ____________ (already/to sell) it in the USA and Canada.

8 After lots of people ____________ (to buy) their ice cream in Britain, they ____________ (to begin) selling it in Japan and Europe.

3 *If*-sentences type 3.

1 Write in the the correct forms of the verbs.

a If I ____________ (to see) you yesterday, I ____________ (to say) hello.

b He ____________ (to get) the job if he ____________ (to go) to the interview.

c If we ____________ (to spend) more money, we ____________ (to get) better seats at the concert.

2 Now complete these sentences. Be careful of negative forms!

a If you ____________ (to get up) earlier, you ____________ (not/ to be) late for your lesson.

b If they ____________ (not/to speak) so quickly, I ____________ (to understand) them better.

c If I ____________ (not/to see) it with my own eyes, I ____________ (not/to believe) it.

d I ____________ (not/to watch) the film, if I ____________ (to know) how boring it was.

e She ____________ (to buy) it if it ____________ (not/to be) so expensive.

If-Sätze Typ 3

Wie alle *if*-Sätze bestehen auch die *if*-Sätze Typ 3 aus zwei Teilen: dem *if*-Teil und dem Hauptsatz.

if-Satz	Hauptsatz
*If I **had seen** you yesterday,*	*I **would have said** hello.*

In *if*-Sätzen Typ 3 sind oft beide Teile verneint. Beachte die Formen:

If …	*I **wouldn't have** …*
*I **hadn't** …*	*he/she/it **wouldn't have** …*
*he/she/it **hadn't** …*	
*we/you/they **hadn't** …*	*we/you/they **wouldn't have** …*

4 *If*-sentences type 3. Read the short text about Bill and Perry then make sentences about them.

Bill and Perry's ice cream is now well-known everywhere. But – as with all businesses – that is only because things happened as they did. It would have been very different, if certain things hadn't happened. In fact, the two men's first business idea wasn't to sell ice cream at all – it was to sell pizza! Just think about the following possibilities …

1 if/Bill and Perry/not/to be at high school together/not/to become friends

If Bill and Perry hadn't been at high school together, they ______

2 if/they/not/to become friends/not/to start a company together

______

3 if/they/to decide to make pizza/they/not/to invent/their famous ice cream

______

4 if/people in their town/to hate/their ice cream/Bill and Perry/to close their shop

______

5 they/not/to open their factory/if/they/to close/their shop

______

6 they/not/to sell/ice cream/all over America/if/not/to open/their factory

______

7 and/they/not/to become successful/in Europe/if/not/to be successful/in the USA

______

Vocabulary

5 New verbs with *to give* and *to put*. Read the Tips and tricks box, then finish the sentences below and on the next page with the right prepositions – *away, out, up* etc.

1 The firemen put ______ the fire.

2 Today we have a class test. Sam, could you give ______ the papers, please?

3 Could I speak to Jenny Clark, please? – One moment, please. I'm putting you ______ now.

Phrasal verbs

Viele häufig vorkommende, kurze Verben bekommen im Englischen eine neue Bedeutung, wenn man ein zweites Wort (meist eine Präposition) ergänzt. Zwei dieser Verben sind *to put* und *to give*. Beispiele:

*to give **away***	*verschenken*
*to give **out***	*verteilen*
*to give **up***	*aufgeben*
*to put sth **off***	*etw verschieben*
*to put **on** (clothes)*	*(Kleidung) anziehen*
*to put **out** (a fire)*	*(ein Feuer) löschen*
*to put sb **through***	*jmdn durchstellen*
*to put **up with** sth*	*etw dulden*

Kickoff Upgrade

Workbook mit Lösungsheft

Klett

Lösungen

Unit 1: Tomorrow's world

Grammar

1 1d, 2b, 3f, 4c, 5a, 6e

2
3 touch
4 will change
5 change
6 will come back
7 come
8 will run
9 will go
10 is
11 leave
12 will touch
13 look
14 will see
15 will go
16 are
17 will change
18 touch
19 are
20 will arrest

Vocabulary

3 **Down**
1 incredibly
2 printer
3 disappear
8 reduce
10 effect
13 destroy
15 space
17 brain

Across
4 climate change
5 virtual
6 solar
7 clean fuels
9 melt
11 human being
12 rainforest
13 double
14 explore
16 power
17 by
18 giant

4
2 dark
3 dirty
4 warmer/hotter
5 safe
6 difficult/hard
7 slower
8 far
9 poor
10 biggest/largest
11 to disappear
12 real

5
1 Unless we find new forms of energy, …
2 Unless we stop global warming, …
3 Unless our lives change, …

Writing

6
1 and
2 also
3 too
4 but
5 In fact,
6 That means that
7 of course
8 for example

Video lounge

7 *Es tut mir so leid! Es tut mir wirklich sehr leid!*
Ach, komm! Der nächste Kaffee geht auf mich.
Du machst Witze, richtig?
Ich bewundere dich und Greg wirklich.
Deshalb hat er das Jahr zwischen Schule und Studium …
Und du, du hast es geschafft, einen Praktikumsplatz zu bekommen
Aber ich habe immer gedacht, …
…, nur um auf der sicheren Seite zu sein.
So kann ich mir einige neue Fertigkeiten aneignen …
… ich habe einen Termin gemacht …
… mit einem Berufsberater/einer Berufsberaterin, …
Das Leben bringt mich um!

Unit 2: Travelling for work

Grammar

1 1
d which
e who
f who
g who
i who, who
j who, who
k who
m which
n who, who

2

NATIONALITY	Norwegian	Austrian
HOUSE COLOUR	yellow	blue
DRINK	water	tea
SPORT	football	golf
PET	cats	horses

NATIONALITY	Brit	German	American
HOUSE COLOUR	red	green	white
DRINK	milk	coffee	chocolate
SPORT	tennis	basketball	squash
PET	birds		dogs

3
(The man who has a fish as a pet is the) German.

2

Down		Across	
1	(which), registration	1	who, receptionist
2	who, passenger	4	which, brochure
3	where, security	7	who, businessman
5	which, key	9	single
6	which, baggage	12	which, which, boarding
8	clerk	13	which, passport
10	where, gate	15	where, desk, desk
11	customs		
14	adult		

Writing

3 2; 16-17 October; near the city centre (if possible); swimming pool (would be great)

4 the Belmont Hotel, it is near the city centre (is in downtown Chicago) and it has a swimming pool.

5
1 16 to 17 October
2 Single
3 Non-smoking
4 Mr Rosenberg
5 (R-)O-S-E-N-B-E-R-G
6 Star Communications

6
1 Reservations, Belmont Hotel, Chicago, Il.
2 Confirmation of telephone reservation
3 Leonie Koch, Star Communications GmbH & Co, Germany
4 made today by telephone
5 Dates:
6 Room:
7 Please note that

Video lounge

7
1
b *sich seinen Lebensunterhalt (mit ...) verdienen*
c *gute Berufsaussichten, Karrierechancen*
d *(deinen / Ihren Fähigkeiten und Interessen) entsprechen; zu (deinen / Ihren Fähigkeiten und Interessen) passen*
e *(einem Verein, Klub) angehören*
f *(deine / Ihre) Stärken*
g *(mit Leuten) umgehen, zu tun haben mit*
h *alphabetische (Jobliste)*
i *Stellenbeschreibung, Tätigkeitsbeschreibung*
j *eine der Hauptaufgaben eines / einer ...*

3 *Individuelle Lösung*

Unit 3: Apprenticeships

Grammar

2
1 Canada
2 had, would be
3 would be, Australia, had
4 would rescue people in the mountains
5 would make, were
6 were, would travel all over Australia

3
1 (If I was a mountain rescue worker in Canada, I would work in the) Rocky Mountains.
2 (If) I worked in a deli in New York, I would work very quickly.
3 (If) I drove a road train in Australia, I would sleep in my lorry (at night).

Vocabulary

4
2 fully qualified
3 information
4 contact
5 looking for
6 part time
7 Hours
8 skills
9 experience
10 careers@techno...com

5 2a, 3b, 4f, 5e, 6g, 7i, 8h, 9c

6

Down		Across	
2	straight away	1	tradespeople
3	subject	5	experienced
4	apply for	8	opportunity
6	currently	10	free time
7	advice	11	ability
9	traineeship	12	fluent
13	tongue	14	attendant
15	take	17	GCSE
16	wage		

Writing

7 *Individuelle Lösung*

9 *Mögliche Lösung*
(Student's home address)

Ms J. Bridges
Laroche Pharma Deutschland
Rehinstraße 2-4
60316 Frankfurt am Main

(date)

Dear Ms Bridges

Traineeship

I am writing to apply for one of the traineeships which you advertised (this week) on the Lehrstellen...de website. I am interested in a traineeship as an office administrative assistant.

I am currently a full-time student at a vocational college in ... (city / town). I will complete my course next year (and hope to get a qualification). I enclose my CV.
Earlier this year I worked for two weeks in an office in my hometown. I am keen to learn, work hard, and my English is good. I would very much welcome the opportunity to work for you as a trainee.

I look forward to hearing from you soon.

Yours sincerely

(name)
(name)

Enc.

Video lounge

10
1 Don't freak out!
2 (Name) speaking
3 See you then!
4 Come in!
5 Please sit down
6 work placement
7 Fine. Go on.
8 Sounds good to me!
9 First of all
10 around the clock
11 (is there) anything else?
12 no matter what happens
13 one possibility would be
14 normally
15 I didn't mean it like that
16 of course not
17 Congratulations!

Unit 4: A visit to a company

Grammar

1
2 carefully, vorsichtig
3 exactly, genau
4 quickly, schnell
5 quietly, ruhig
6 slowly, langsam
7 urgently, dringend
8 (inter)nationally, (inter)national
9 centrally, zentral
10 locally, örtlich, lokal
11 punctually, pünktlich
12 (un)usually, (un)gewöhnlich
13 politely, höflich
14 angrily, verärgert, wütend
15 easily, leicht, problemlos
16 happily, fröhlich, glücklich
17 healthily, gesund
18 hungrily, hungrig
19 noisily, geräuschsvoll
20 fashionably, modisch
21 reasonably, vernünftig
22 simply, einfach
23 terribly, schrecklich
24 automatically, automatisch
25 basically, grundsätzlich
26 dramatically, dramatisch
27 well, gut

2
2 healthy, healthily
3 internationally, international
4 well, good
5 quiet, quietly
6 fashionably, fashionable
7 locally, local
8 simple, simply

3
2 carefully
3 quick
4 politely
5 exact
6 easily
7 slowly
8 hungrily

Vocabulary

4
1 Bereich
2 Versand
3 Eingang
4 Labor
5 Lastwagen, LKW
6 Büros
7 verarbeiten, bearbeiten
8 Produkt
9 Produktion
10 Qualitätskontrolle
11 Rohmaterialien
12 Forschung und Entwicklung
13 erfinden
14 beladen, laden
15 lagern
16 Lager

2 invent
3 raw materials
4 to store
5 production
6 warehouse
7 quality control
8 offices
9 loads

5 **Down**

1 report
2 manufacturer
3 DIY
4 nice
5 by the way
9 technician
10 head office
14 to grow
15 sorts

Across

6 appointment
7 introduce
8 entrance
11 apprentice
12 this way
13 to imagine
16 around

Writing

6 *Mögliche Lösung*

Hi (name)

(This week I'm in England! I'm here with) three other students and our trainer from college. Today we visited a paint factory and we spoke to some of the workers there. It was very interesting, particularly the laboratory. We are staying at a small hotel. This is my first visit to England and it's fascinating. I have to speak lots of English and that's hard, but I think my English is improving. The weather here is a bit wet! I always heard English food is bad but it's nice! Yesterday we had fish and chips! Delicious!

Your friend
(name)

Video lounge

7
1 to stay with us
2 twenty-fourth
3 twenty-first
4 twenty-fourth
5 twenty-fourth
6 Cheng
7 Xiao
8 single, a twin, or a double room

Unit 5: Global business

Grammar

1
2 are bought
3 are bought
4 are stored
5 are transported
6 are (often) delivered
7 are bought
8 are put
9 is used

2
1 (was invented by) Native Americans.
2 (were) invented by a German scientist.
3 was made in Egypt.
4 was discovered about 2,000 years ago in Mexico.

3
2 These computer screens are manufactured in Japan.
3 My new computer was delivered yesterday.
4 Our products are bought worldwide.
5 English is spoken in many / lots of countries.
6 Many / Lots of new buildings were built in the sixties / 1960s.
7 Our products are not sold in the USA.
8 The boy was (only) paid (only) one euro for his work.

4 **Down**

1 earn
2 helpline
3 manufacture
4 call centre
5 mine
8 world market
9 assemble
10 produce
15 sold
17 bought
18 grown

Across

6 hard drive
7 tower
11 Silicon Valley
12 on sale
13 bakery
14 expensive
16 deliver
19 order
20 CPU

Writing

5 A 2j, 3g, 4k, 5l, 6b, 7i, 8h, 9e, 10d, 11a, 12f

C *Mögliche Lösung*
(First, the tomatoes are harvested and they are transported to the factory by trucks. Only the very best quality tomatoes are used to manufacture ketchup. In the factory) the tomatoes are (first) washed, chopped and pre-cooked in big metal vats. Then, they are pulped by pulping machines and the skins and seeds are removed. Next, the tomatoes are cooked in big cooking tanks. Spices are added, too. After that, it is necessary to remove the air in the ketchup and this is done by aerating tanks. Finally, the ketchup is bottled. The ketchup is kept at a temperature of 90º while it is bottled – this kills any bacteria. And now you have ketchup!

Video lounge

6
1 calling
2 credit card
3 number
4 1010 2237 6849 6464
5 (04/14)
6 We look forward to

Unit 6: A month in New Zealand

Grammar

1 *Point in time (Zeitpunkt)*
2 last Monday
3 the beginning of June
4 I was small
5 2010
6 23 January
7 yesterday
8 I started at college

Period of time (Zeitraum)
b a (very) long time!
c 20 minutes
d four hours
e three months
f ages
g six days
h two weeks

2 *Mögliche Lösung*
2 since 8 o'clock / for 20 minutes.
3 for three months
4 since I was small
5 for ages / for a very long time
6 since I started at college / for ten years
7 since yesterday

3
2 worked
3 bought
4 has been
5 had
6 grew
7 took over
8 decided
9 has produced
10 has helped
11 left
12 has been

Vocabulary

4
2 PURCHASING
3 PRODUCTION
4 QUALITY CONTROL
5 MARKETING
6 SALES
7 DISTRIBUTION (LOGISTICS)
8 ACCOUNTS
9 HUMAN RESOURCES (HR)

Accounts	*Buchhaltung*
Distribution	*Vertrieb*
Human resources	*Personalabteilung*
Marketing	*Marketing*
Production	*Produktion*
Purchasing	*Einkauf*
Quality control	*Qualitätskontrolle*
Sales	*Verkauf*

5
2 hairdresser
3 office worker
4 manager
5 mechanic
6 electrician
7 technician
8 engineer
9 doctor
10 film director
11 supervisor
12 author
13 scientist
14 psychologist
15 therapist

Writing

6 *Mögliche Lösung*
A (No thanks.) (I'm afraid) I'm absolutely full up.
B Thank you.
C Sure / Of course.
D Oh right, I understand now.
E That would be great.

7
1 Excuse me. Could you help me, please?
2 How are you this morning?
3 Yes, please. They're delicious.

8
2 Could you please let us know when you will arrive at the airport?
3 Could you please tell me the name of that nice hotel near the railway station?
4 Could you please let me have your report next week?

Video lounge

9 1 *Mögliche Lösung*

Florence Hi! I'm Florence. (*Das klingt, als müsste jeder wissen, wer sie ist – das wirkt sehr überheblich.*)

Florence Sure! That's why I'm here, honey! (*Sarkastisch, sie nennt Maya* honey. *Man benutzt dieses Wort nicht für fremde Personen.*)

Florence Are you kidding? (*Das klingt so, als halte sie Maya für dumm. Das ist sehr unhöflich.*) You don't know who I am?

Florence Hi! Fine, thanks. (*Nicole ist freundlich, aber die Reaktion von Florence ist gelangweilt und unfreundlich.*) I just came from home – that's Texas (*sie erklärt Texas so, als würde sie mit einem Kind sprechen*) – to promote my new perfume here in Berlin.

Maya Yes, Ms Ryam. We have reserved the Ambassador Suite for you. Here's your room key. (*Florence bedankt sich nicht, als Maya ihr den Schlüssel gibt.*)

Florence I usually have breakfast at 12. (*Wieder reagiert Florence so, als müsste jeder wissen, was sie für Gewohnheiten hat. Das Frühstück zu einer anderen Zeit zu*

	erwarten, ist schwierig in einem Hotel.)
Florence	You mean the 2nd floor. (*Florence korrigiert Maya so, als hätte sie einen dummen Fehler gemacht.*)
Florence	Yeah, right. Whatever. (*Florence Antwort ist unverschämt.* Whatever *bedeutet, es interessiert mich nicht, was jemand sagt.*) Porter? Come on! (Come on! *ist ein klarer Befehl. Man würde im Englischen niemals so mit jemandem sprechen, etwa einem Türsteher oder einem Mitarbeiter an der Rezeption. Höflich wäre:* Could you please take me to my room now?)
Maya	Enjoy your stay with us! (*Florence antwortet Maya nicht. Das wirkt so, als wäre sie zu unwichtig.*)

2 *Mögliche Lösung*
Berlin, hotel reception

Maya	Hi! Welcome to the Ryam Hotel! How can I help you?
Florence	Hi! I'm Florence Ryam, my grandfather owns this hotel. I have a reservation.
Maya	Oh hello, Ms Ryam. Welcome to the hotel.
Florence	Thank you. It's nice to be here.
Nicole	Hello, Ms Ryam. How are you?
Florence	Hi, Nicole. I'm fine thanks. I'm just here in Berlin to promote my new perfume. How are you?
Nicole	Fine, thank you. That's really interesting. I hope it all goes well.
Florence	Thanks!
Maya	So, Ms Ryam, we have reserved the Ambassador Suite for you. Here's your room key.
Florence	Thanks.
Maya	Our porter will be more than happy to take up all your luggage for you. Oh, Ms Ryam? Breakfast is served from 6 until 10 o'clock on the first floor.
Florence	I usually have breakfast at 12. Would that be OK with you?
Maya	Of, course.
Florence	And I'm a bit confused, sorry. Why do you serve breakfast down here?
Maya	Down here? No, it's one floor above us.
Florence	Of, I understand now. You're from Britain, right? In the USA we say the 'first floor' for the 'ground floor'.
Maya	Sorry! I'll remember that!
Florence	No problem. OK, porter, could you take me to my room now?
Maya	Enjoy your stay with us.
Florence	Thank you. I'm sure I will.

Unit 7: My job is special

Grammar

1
1 they had finished high school
2 they had already gone to live in Vermont
3 they had decided to start an ice cream business
4 they had learned how to make ice cream

2
1 had opened, became
2 opened, had become
3 had already become, opened
4 had become, decided
5 started, had been
6 could, had built
7 started, had already sold
8 had bought, began

3
1
a had seen, would have said
b would have got, had gone
c had spent, would have got

2
a had got up, wouldn't have been
b hadn't spoken, would have understood
c hadn't seen, wouldn't have believed
d wouldn't have watched, had known
e would have bought, hadn't been

4
1 …, wouldn't have become friends.
2 If they hadn't become friends, they wouldn't have started a company together.
3 If they had decided to make pizza, they wouldn't have invented their famous ice cream.
4 If people in their town had hated their ice cream, Bill and Perry would have closed their shop.
5 They wouldn't have opened their factory if they had closed their shop.
6 Thy wouldn't have sold ice cream all over America if they hadn't opened their factory.
7 And they wouldn't have become successful in Europe if they hadn't been successful in the USA.

Vocabulary

5
1 out
2 out
3 through
4 up
5 on
6 away
7 off
8 up with

6 1

Down	**Across**
1 homeless	3 glad
2 absolutely	4 neighbour
3 graph	5 set fire to
8 vacation	6 hold
9 hose	7 vehicle
10 engineer	10 emergency
11 nearby	12 check
12 coast	13 amazing
	14 popular

2

1 vehicle	5 glad
2 absolutely	6 popular
3 emergency	7 nearby
4 set fire to	8 homeless

Writing

7 *Mögliche Lösung*

I'm a college student and right now I'm looking for a part-time job. Two weeks ago, I was in town and I saw an advertisement in the window of a sports shop: 'Wanted: part-time sales assistant'. It looked perfect. I went in, got a form, filled it in, and gave it to the manager. He looked pleased and said: "That seems great. I think we can give you the job but I'll phone you later in the week." On Friday morning, I was on the bus on the way to college when my phone rang. It was the manager. "I'm sorry," he said, "but we don't need you for the part-time job." I was really surprised. "But why?" I asked, "You said …" "One word," the manager said. *"Myface."* I have a page on the social networking site *myface*. And then I remembered. Three weeks ago my friend was 18 and he had a party. I drank too much alcohol and put a photo of myself on my page. I won't say much about the photo but it wasn't good. The manager had looked at my page and he had seen the photo. I felt so stupid. If I hadn't put that photo on my page, I know I would have got the job. So remember: think before you post pictures. Other people can see them!
(226 words)

Video lounge

8 1

to agree – *zustimmen*
colourful – *bunt*
classy – *stilvoll*
high impact plastic – *stoßfester Kunststoff*
affordable – *bezahlbar*
consumer camera – *Verbraucherkamera*
underwater – *Unterwasser-*
deep – *tief*
guarantee – *Garantie*
waterproof – *wasserfest*
up to – *bis zu*
foot/feet – *Fuß*
power consumption – *Stromverbrauch*
to be supplied with – *wird geliefert mit*
rechargeable battery – *(aufladbarer) Akku*
charger – *Ladegerät*
to be concerned – *besorgt sein*
to appeal to sb – *jmdm gefallen*
market (for a product) – *Markt (für ein Produkt)*
compeltely different – *vollkommen anders*
taste – *Geschmack*
universal – *universell*
stylish – *elegant*
definitely – *bestimmt*

3
Mögliche Lösung
The new Okonai 45 camera is both stylish and practical. Made of high impact plastic, the camera can also be used underwater up to at least two meters deep. Its power consumption is good, too. Every camera is supplied with two long-life rechargeable batteries and a charger. Young people will definitely love this camera because it is affordable and classy. The camera is already a big hit in China. It will soon become just as popular in Europe.
(78 words)

Unit 8: Starting work

Grammar

1

2 I like / enjoy	4 I don't like / dislike
3 I don't mind	5 hate / can't stand

2 *Mögliche Lösung*
1 (I love) listening to my favourite band.
2 I enjoy going to a fitness club and cycling.
3 I don't mind doing homework.
4 I don't like tidying my room or washing up.
5 I can't stand doing nothing.

3

1 to see	5 to work
2 being	6 being
3 living	7 to see
4 to go	

4

2 learn	6 forget
3 expect	7 promised
4 hope	8 try
5 afford	9 decided

5
2 suggested
3 There's no point in / It's no good
4 miss
5 practise
6 that means

6
2 to give
3 to be
4 to go / going
5 waiting
6 to walk
7 to rain / raining
8 to explain
9 to be
10 to have
11 working
12 trying
13 sitting
14 to fall

Vocabulary

7
2 to do
3 made
4 do
5 do
6 to do
7 to make
8 do
9 to make

8
Across
1 enthusiastic
7 impression
8 reliable
10 brilliant
12 warehouse
13 retail
15 traffic
16 chain
18 get on with
19 solve
20 deliver

Down
2 till
3 advertising
4 complicated
5 display
6 on time
9 workplace
11 logistics
14 mentor
17 tired

Writing

9 *Mögliche Lösung*
(Paul / Paula likes) working in the restaurant.
((S)he particularly enjoys) serving customers.
(But (s)he dislikes) cleaning tables.
(Every day (s)he learns) to do something new.
((S)he loves the job but misses) having free time at the weekends.
(One day, (s)he would like) to train to be a chef.
((S)he) would like maybe to have her own restaurant or café.
((S)he) also loves earning money.

Paula has just started work in a restaurant in the town where she lives. She likes working there and she particularly enjoys serving customers. She often chats to them and sometimes her friends come into the restaurant. But Paula doesn't like cleaning tables – they are sometimes a terrible mess! The restaurant is great because every day she learns something new. Does Paula miss anything now that she has a full-time job? Yes, she sometimes has to work on Saturday and Sunday and she misses having her free time at the weekends. Paula likes being a waitress but one day she would like to train to be a chef. She would like maybe to have her own restaurant or café in town. Paula has to work hard but there is one very good thing – she loves earning money.

Video lounge

10 *Mögliche Lösung*
2 Nicole gives some flowers to Maya.
3 Nicole gives Maya a box / a camera from Mr Xiao.
4 Maya opens the box and sees the camera.
5 Nicole gives Maya an envelope / a hotel voucher.
6 Nicole reads (aloud) the letter of recommendation.
7 Maya embraces / hugs Nicole
8 The porter puts the cake on the table.
9 (Maya) cuts the cake / a piece of cake.
10 Maya gives a piece / a slice of cake to Nicole.

Unit 9: Working in an office

Grammar

1 1
... she lived at 1214 Palos Park, Chicago. She said that she didn't know why Mr Young was dead. She said that she was innocent.
... he lived at 25 Willmington Road, Chicago. He said that he was Mr Young's boss but (that) he was not a killer.

3
1 Andrea said that their server had been a young woman with red hair but Todd said that their server had been a young man.
2 Angel said that there had been no music in the restaurant but Todd said that there had been some sort of quiet Italian music.
3 Angel said that they had seen two friends in the restaurant but that they hadn't spoken to them. Todd said that the two friends had come to their table to say 'hello'.
4 Angel said that they had talked about baseball but Todd said they hadn't talked about it/baseball.
5 Angel said that Todd had taken a taxi home but Todd said that he had taken an Orange Line train (and had then walked).

Vocabulary

2 1

a to answer – the phone
b to go to/to attend – meetings
c to meet/to welcome/to look after – visitors
d to read/to write/to send/to reply to – emails
e to start/to finish – work
f to take messages

2

1 start	6 write/send
2 finish	7 attend/go to
3 answer	8 meet/welcome
4 take	9 look after
5 read	

3

Down	Across
1 multinational	3 business lunch
2 client	5 head office
3 boss	6 Silicon Valley
4 sales manager	9 meeting
6 companies	10 PA
8 factories	11 representative
14 call	12 diary
	13 logistics
	15 look after

Writing

4 … there were lots of other producers of fruit drinks. He thought that we needed something different form the ordinary ads. ES said that she agreed. Fruit drinks were always 'healthy' in ads. She added that people saw families in the sunshine, blue sky, etc. ER answered that that was right, but not bad. He said that people bought fruit drinks because they were healthy. He explained that they compared them with colas and other drinks with lots of sugar. JA pointed out that 'healthy' didn't have to mean 'boring'.

Video lounge

5 2

on time – *rechtzeitig*
Like what? – *Wie was?*
stuff – *Zeug, Kram*
I guess. – *Ich vermute.*
way too much – *viel zu viel*
Really? – *Wirklich?*
not to mention – *nicht zu bemerken*
I know what you mean. – *Ich weiß, was du meinst.*
really nice – *wirklich nett*
Of course not! – *Natürlich nicht!*
Time will tell. – *Die Zeit wird es zeigen.*
But enough about … – *Aber genug über …*

Anhang

A company profile

A
2 It makes headphones, microphones and aviation headsets.
3 Its headquarters are in Hannover, Germany.
4 Dr Karl Weissheimer founded the company in 1945.
5 Its turnover last year was 584.4 million EUR.
6 The company has 2,326 employees in total.
7 Of these, 1,223 work in Germany and 1,103 work abroad.
8 The company's CEO at the moment is Dr Martin Weissheimer.
9 It has factories in the USA, Ireland and Germany.
10 It has sales offices in 14 countries outside Germany.

B

Down	Across
1 employee	4 abroad
2 family-owned	5 found
3 manufacturer	7 sales office
6 turnover	8 factory
	9 worldwide
	10 headquarters

Business correspondence 1: an enquiry

1
1 Finding a new business partner
2 An enquiry
3 An offer
4 An order

2

2 goods	14 discount
3 supplier	15 within
4 to supply	16 terms of payment
5 manufacturer	17 quality
6 to manufacture	18 sample
7 business partner	19 offer
8 advertisement	20 to include
9 trade magazine	21 to be satisfied
10 trade fair	22 to place an order
11 enquiry	23 order form
12 consumer	24 catalogue number
13 price	25 to dispatch

Business correspondence 2: an offer

2

2	(FAS)	€1,150
3	(FOB)	€1,160
4	(CFR)	€1,360
5	(DEQ)	€1,370
6	(DDP)	€1,470

Business correspondence 3: an order

1

Down
1 competitive
2 enquiry
3 current
6 attached
7 discounts
8 sincerely
9 purchase
11 further
14 require
15 valid
17 offer

Across
4 catalogue
5 in full
9 price list
10 transfer
12 receipt
13 forward
16 volume
18 item
19 enclosed

2

Enquiries
2 website
3 (large) quantities
4 discounts

Orders
13 offer / letter / email
14 note
15 require

Offers
5 enquiry
6 following
7 prices
8 offer
9 payment
10 dispatch
11 valid
12 order

3 2g, 3i, 4b, 5c, 6e, 7f, 8d, 9a

Business correspondence 4: a complaint

1 (Mistakes in commerce often have to do with) (sending) goods
(Problem 1:) (a delay in) delivery
(Problem 2:) goods arrive damaged
(Problem 3:) supplier sends the wrong goods
(Problem 4:) goods are faulty / defective
(A mistake is important but) how you put it right is even more important

2

Email 1
Supplier sends the wrong goods.

Email 2
Goods arrive damaged.

Email 3
A delay in delivery.

Email 4
Goods are faulty / defective.

Writing an advertisement

1 The best in town since 1995
2 11 Market Place
Danbury
3 Are you tired of eating cold pizza?
4 We deliver FAST!
5 (Paragraph 1) When you order a pizza you want it fast. And hot. But sometimes when it arrives it looks and tastes like an old shoe!
(Paragraph 2) Not a Luigi's pizza! If you live in Danbury, we GUARANTEE delivery in 20 minutes OR YOUR MONEY BACK! That's right. No pizza in 20 minutes and you pay nothing.
(Paragraph 3) Isn't it time you got your pizzas hot? Call us TODAY on
6 (01299) 414414
7 LUIGI'S PIZZAS – THE BEST IN TOWN SINCE 1995!!

Kickoff Upgrade Workbook

Dieses Lösungsheft ist Bestandteil von:

ISBN 978-3-12-**808304**-9

4 My first week at work was really hard. I almost gave ____________ and left.

5 She had a shower, put ____________ her clothes, and went to work.

6 The shop is giving ____________ free T-shirts this week.

7 I want to go on a diet but every day I put it ____________.

8 You mustn't put ____________ a situation at work which is unfair. Tell somebody about it and find a solution.

6 Try this crossword. All the words were in the unit.

1 Write in the answers to the crossword.
2 Complete the sentences with the correct words.

Down

1 a person who doesn't have a place to live is … (*heimatslos*)
2 I'm sorry, I don't know at all – I have … no idea!
3 This … shows how much the company earned each month last year. (*Diagramm*)
8 the American English word for holiday
9 firefighters use these to put out fires (*Schlauch*)
10 IngenieurIn
11 not far away (*nebenan*)
12 New York city is on the east … of America (*Küste*)

Across

3 I'm … that you like it. (*Es freut mich, dass …*)
4 a person who lives near you (*Nachbar*)
5 to …: *anzünden, in Brand setzen* (3 words)
6 to … : *halten*. Please … my hand when we cross the road.
7 a car is a kind of … (*Fahrzeug*)
10 In Britain, if there is an …, you call 999 (*Notfall*)
12 to …: *überprüfen*
13 That's …! I can't believe it! (*erstaunlich*)
14 Everybody likes these jeans – they're very … (*beliebt*)

1 She's a ____________ mechanic: she repairs cars.

2 I asked Philip but he had ____________ no idea where Paul lives.

3 Please, can I use your phone? This is an ____________.

4 The man threw down a cigarette and it ____________ the grass.

5 I almost gave up, but now I'm ____________ that I didn't.

6 The most ____________ boy in our class is Tim – we all like him.

7 My flat is great but unfortunately there aren't any shops ____________. I have to go into town if I need to buy something.

8 If I hadn't gone to the hostel I would have become ____________ and would have had to live on the streets.

Writing

7 Look at the two pictures. Choose one and write a short story (you can change the young man to a young woman if you want).

1 Decide if your person is happy (because he or she was successful) or annoyed (because he or she made a bad mistake).
2 Imagine why your person has those feelings and write a story about the events before this picture. You can write the story with I or he/she.
3 End your story with this phrase:
'If I had / hadn't …. I would / wouldn't have …'

Video lounge

8 Describe Mr Xiao's camera.

1 Find and write in the German meanings of the English words and phrases below.
2 Watch the part of the video where Mr Xiao makes a presentation of his camera to the German businessmen.
3 Write a short description of (or an advertisement for) the camera.

bezahlbar stilvoll Ladegerät bunt vollkommen anders Verbraucherkamera Garantie stoßfester Kunststoff Markt (für ein Produkt) tief bestimmt Geschmack Stromverbrauch Fuß (aufladbarer) Akku ~~zustimmen~~ elegant jmdm gefallen bis zu besorgt sein wird geliefert mit universell Unterwasser wasserfest

to agree	zustimmen	power consumption	
colourful		to be supplied with	
classy		rechargeable battery	
high impact plastic		charger	
affordable		to be concerned	
consumer camera		to appeal to sb	
underwater		market (for a product)	
deep		completely different	
guarantee		taste	
waterproof		universal	
up to		stylish	
foot/feet		definitely	

Unit 8 Starting work

Grammar

1 Verbs and phrases plus *-ing*. Write the expressions below into the diagram.

hate/can't stand   love   not mind   like/enjoy   not like/dislike

1 I love ________ 2 ________ 3 ________ 4 ________ 5 ________

2 Use five of the expressions from exercise 1 to write sentences about yourself. Remember: after all these expressions you need an *–ing* form.

1 I love ________________________________
2 ________________________________
3 ________________________________
4 ________________________________
5 ________________________________

3 *Infinitive* or *–ing* form? Complete the sentences with the correct forms.

1 Would you like ________________ (to see) my new laptop?
2 I like ________________ (to be) a college student.
3 Do you like ________________ (to live) here?
4 One day, I'd like ________________ (to go) to China.
5 I wouldn't like ________________ (to work) for your boss.
6 No-one likes ________________ (to be) criticised.
7 I'd really like ________________ (to see) that new film.

Merke!
Nach dem Verb *to like* benutzt man die *ing*-Form:
I like watching old movies.
Aber nach *would like* benutzt man den Infinitiv:
I'd like to go now.

4 Lots of verbs which you use all the time are followed by an *infinitive*. Choose the best verbs to complete these sentences. Use the correct forms of the verbs (*simple present, simple past* etc.)

to afford   to forget   to hope   to decide   to learn   to expect   to want   to promise   to try

1 When I finish my college course I want ________________ to find an apprenticeship with a building firm.
2 When people do an apprenticeship they ________________ to do things in a practical way, often with an experienced tradesperson as their teacher.

Hannah wanted to eat more healthy food but it wasn't always easy.

3 When you first start work you can't __________ to know everything straight away.

4 One day, if all goes well, I __________ to become a manager.

5 I can't __________ to buy a car at the moment because I don't have much money.

6 Don't __________ to turn the lights off* when you leave the office.

7 I had my interview last week. The interviewer __________ to let me know today if I have got the job.

8 In a work situation you must __________ to get on with the people you work with even if it isn't always easy. Conflict is never the answer.

9 James was quite unhappy in his office and after a lot of thought he __________ to look for a new job.

5 All the expressions below are followed by an *-ing* form. Choose the best expressions to finish the sentences. Use the correct forms (*simple present, simple past* etc.)

to imagine to miss that means to suggest to practise there's no point in/it's no good (choose one)

Lewis sometimes closed his eyes and imagined being on a beautiful tropical island.

1 I can't imagine __________ living without the internet.

2 My careers teacher at school __________ doing an apprenticeship. He said I'd 'earn while I learn'.

3 __________ writing to him. He never answers emails.

4 We moved last month to a new town. I love living here but I __________ seeing my old friends.

5 A good way to __________ listening to English is to watch English movies.

6 You want to be successful, right? Well, __________ working hard!

6 *Infinitive* or *-ing* form? The text below is based on a true story. Complete it with the correct forms of the verbs – *infinitive* or *-ing form*. Be careful! In two sentences both answers are possible.

I'LL NEVER FORGET MY FIRST DAY AT WORK!

In my first year at college, I decided **(1)** to get __________ (to get) some work experience. My parents have a friend who is a doctor and she agreed **(2)** __________ (to give) me a job for three weeks in her practice. I didn't want **(3)** __________ (to be) late on my first day, so I got up early, had a good breakfast, and took the bus into town. That's when things started **(4)** __________ (to go) wrong. The bus broke down**! There was no point in **(5)** __________ (to wait) for the next bus, so I decided **(6)** __________ (to walk) to the doctor's practice. It soon began **(7)** __________ (to rain) and when I arrived, I was wet, tired – and 15 minutes late. The practice manager met me and she didn't look friendly. I tried **(8)**

→ * to turn off (lights): *(Lichter) abschalten* → ** to break down: eine Panne haben

__________________ (to explain) about the bus and promised **(9)** __________________ (to be) on time in future but she just pointed to* a desk and said I could start work straight away. I expected **(10)** __________________ (to have) lots of help on my first day, but the manager just went away and left me. On the desk there were lots of letters and forms and other pieces of paper and a note that said: 'Please put these in the filing cabinet** behind you.' I didn't mind **(11)** __________________ (to work) on my own, but I just couldn't understand what to do and after about ten minutes I gave up **(12)** __________________ (to try) to file the papers. Fortunately, a nice receptionist came in then and helped me and after a bit I was busy with the documents. That's when it happened! I mean, that's when the absolute catastrophe happened. Suddenly, the door of the office flew open and three armed*** police officers ran in. Can you imagine **(13)** __________________ (to sit) in an office and the door opens and suddenly there are people with guns? I think I just screamed. Then the practice manager came in and she screamed. Then the doctor came in and she – yes - screamed. The police officers looked confused, too. 'What's the emergency****?' one asked. 'There is no emergency', the practice manager said. 'But we had an alarm at the police station', the officer replied. Then the practice manager looked at me. Nobody had told me, but under my desk there was a panic button***** and I had pushed it with my knee. At that moment, I just wanted **(14)** __________________ (to fall) through a hole in the floor and disappear!

Vocabulary

7 **The verbs *to do* and *to make*. Read the tip box then underline the correct verb in the sentences below. Use your dictionary if you are not sure.**

1 Why do you want *to do* / *to make* an apprenticeship?
2 At the end of this year I have *to do* / *to make* an exam.
3 Sorry, I think I *did* / *made* a mistake.
4 Did you *do* / *make* your homework yesterday?
5 If you *do* / *make* this exercise, you'll learn a lot about the verbs *to do* and *to make.*
6 I have to go early today. I need *to do* / *to make* the shopping before I go home.
7 It isn't always easy *to do* / *to make* decisions.
8 We *do* / *make* a lot of business with a firm in England.
9 I'd like *to do* / *to make* an appointment to see Mrs White, please.

The verbs *to do* and *to make*

Das Verb *to do* wird gewöhnlich benutzt um eine Aktivität zu beschreiben: *What did you do at the weekend?*
Das Verb *to make* wird benutzt, wenn man etwas „baut" oder „herstellt": *Our company makes tyres.*
Es gibt allerdings eine Reihe von feststehenden Ausdrücken im Englischen mit *to do* oder *to make*, wobei jeweils nur ein Ausdruck korrekt ist. Leider gibt es keine klaren Regeln und man muss diese Ausdrücke einzeln lernen.

→ * to point to sth: *auf etw hindeuten* → ** filing cabinet: *Aktenschrank*
→ *** armed: *bewaffnet* → **** emergency: *Notsituation*
→ ***** panic button: *Alarmschalter*

8 **Do the crossword. All the words were in the unit.**

Across

1 *enthusiastisch*
7 He made a good … *Eindruck*
8 Employers like people who are … *zuverlässig*
10 *glänzend!*
12 a place where goods are stored *Lagerhalle*
13 *Einzelhandel*
15 The … was bad this morning. *Verkehr*
16 Our store is part of a national …. *Kette*
18 to … people = *(mit Menschen) gut auskommen* (3 words)
19 Try to … this problem. *lösen*
20 to … = *liefern*

Down

2 *Ladenkasse*
3 … and marketing *Werbung*
4 *kompliziert*
5 I like your window …. *Schaufenster*
6 Get to work … - don't be late! *rechtzeitig* (2 words)
9 *Arbeitsplatz*
11 *Logistik*
14 Apprentices usually have a …. *Vertrauensperson*
17 I didn't sleep well last night and today I feel… *müde*

Writing

9 **Paul/Paula is a young British person who has just started work in a restaurant. Complete the table below about her/him with your own ideas, then use the table to write a short text about Paul/Paula. Write on a separate piece of paper.**

Paul / Paula likes	working in the restaurant.
(S)he particularly enjoys	
But (s)he dislikes	
Every day (s)he learns	
(S)he loves the job but misses	
One day, (s)he would like	
(S)he	
(S)he	

Video lounge

10 Watch the video and write in directions (*Regieanweisungen*). Remember that in English these are always in the *simple present*.

Nicole **(1)** Nicole and the others enter the room. There she is!

Maya What is going on?

Nicole Well, you didn't think we'd forget it's your last day, did you? **(2)** ____________________

Maya Well, I definitely wasn't expecting anything like this!

Nicole Well, we'd just like you to know that we've all been very happy with your work here. And you've been a great help at reception. And, yeah, even some of the guests have said some very complimentary things about you.

Maya Oh, really? Which guests?

Nicole Well, Florence Ryam mentioned that you helped her out. And –

Maya No!

Nicole And you can really pride yourself on that. We all know how difficult she can be. And our guest from China said that with your help he managed to clinch a big deal with a major German customer.

Maya Oh, I'm so pleased Mr Xiao's presentation went well!

Nicole Yes. And he was so grateful that he left you a gift. **(3)** ____________________

Maya **(4)** ____________________ Oh, my goodness!

Nicole And we have a little something here for you, too. **(5)** ____________________ It's a hotel voucher. You can use it at any of our hotels.

Maya Oh, thank you so much!

Nicole And we have your letter of recommendation here. **(6)** ____________________ OK: "well organised" … "driven in equal measure both by quality and efficiency" … "Maya was always punctual". … "I have no hesitation in recommending Maya Conway for any position relating to the hotel industry".

Maya Thank you so much, Nicole!

Nicole Well, I hope it helps you out in the future. And thank you so much for your dedication and we'd be more than delighted to have you back here again – and on our staff, of course.

Maya Oh, come on, you! **(7)** ____________________ Thank you! Come on, guys, lets tuck into the cake!

Porter **(8)** ____________________ Bitteschön!

Maya Oh, it looks so good! Shall I do the honours?

Nicole Yes, please!

Porter Of course.

Nicole **(9)** Maya ____________________ Yeah, we heard you like chocolate.

Maya Oh, wow!

Nicole **(10)** Maya ____________________ Oh, my goodness, that's a huge piece!

Die Verwendung von *to give*

Man verwendet *to give* oft in Wendungen wie *to give sth to sb* (jmdm etw geben). Man kann das mit oder ohne *to* ausdrücken, muss aber auf die richtige Wortstellung achten.
*Nicole gives (1) the flowers **to** (2) Maya.*
Oder: *Nicole gives (1) Maya (2) the flowers.*

Unit 9 Working in an office

Grammar

1 ***Indirect speech.*** **In this task, you will help a detective with a murder. Read about the murder and the people involved below.**

At 7.30 this morning, office workers in downtown Chicago found a dead body. It was one of their colleagues, Jack Young. He had died at around 9 pm the evening before. Detective Victor Santiago suspected* two people who also worked in the office: Angel Grant and Todd Friedman. He arrested** them and took them to police headquarters.

Angel Grant
I live at 1214 Palos Park, Chicago. I don't know why Mr Young is dead. I'm innocent!

Todd Friedman
I live at 25 Willmington Road, Chicago. I'm Mr Young's boss but I'm not a killer!

1 This is what the two people said when they were arrested. Write their words below in indirect speech.

Angel Grant said that she ______________________________

____

____

Todd Friedman told Detective Santiago that ______________________________

____

____

→ * to suspect sb: *jmdn verdächtigen* → ** to arrest sb: *jmdn festnehmen*

2 Angel and Todd said that they had an alibi for the time of the murder: they had been together all evening. Detective Santiago decided to question them separately*, first Angel, then Todd.

- Read what Angel and Todd said below.
- Did they both say the same things or are there differences between their statements**? If there are, then maybe they weren't together!
- Find any differences you can and underline them in the statements.
- Now explain why the two statements are different. For example: *Angel said that they had … but Todd said that they had …*

3 Write out the differences below. (Tip: there are five!)

ANGEL GRANT	TODD FRIEDMAN
I left work yesterday evening at about 5.30. I went home, phoned my mom and had a cup of coffee. At around 7 pm, I left home and took a taxi to West 123rd Street. There's a pizzeria there called Luigi's. I went in, sat down, and ordered a glass of red wine. Todd arrived ten minutes later. That was at around 8 pm. We ordered our food straight away. I ordered Spaghetti Carbonara and a green salad. Todd ordered a pizza with peperoni. Our server*** was a young woman with red hair called Andrea. We ate our meal and then we both ordered ice cream. There was no music in the restaurant. It was quite busy and we saw two friends there that we knew but we didn't speak to them. We talked about work for a bit, about baseball – we both like the Chicago White Sox – and about Todd's new apartment. We left the restaurant at about 9.30 pm. It was a nice evening, so we walked in the park for about half and hour, then I took a taxi home. Todd took a taxi, too. And that was how we both spent our evening. We didn't go to the office and we didn't kill Jack Young!	I worked late yesterday evening and didn't leave the office until around 7.30. I didn't go home, I took a taxi and went straight to West 123rd Street to meet Angel at a pizzeria there called Luigi's. I guess I arrived there at about 8 pm. We ordered our food as soon as I arrived. I had a pizza with peperoni and Angel had Spaghetti Carbonara with a green salad, I think. Our server? I'm not sure. I think it was a young man. Anyway, we ate our meal and then we both ordered ice cream. Was there any music in the restaurant? Yes, there was some sort of quiet Italian music. The restaurant was quite busy and we saw two friends there that we knew. Hmm, yes, they came to our table and said 'hello'. We talked about work, about baseball and about my new apartment. We left the restaurant at about 9.30 pm. It was a nice evening so we walked in the park for half an hour, then Angel took a taxi home. How did I go home? Hmm, I took an Orange Line train, then I walked. We didn't go to the office and we didn't kill Jack Young!

1 *Angel said that* ______________________

____

____

____

____

____

____

____

____

____

____

____

→ *separately: *einzeln* → **statement: *Aussage* → ***server (AE): *Kellner*

Vocabulary

2 In an office. Alicia Kerr works for an advertising agency in San Francisco. Her boss is Mr Landry. Look at the picture and do the tasks below.

1 Find and write in the words which complete the table.

emails meetings messages the phone visitors work

a	to answer	
b	to go to / to attend	
c	to meet / to welcome / to look after	
d	to read / to write / to send / to reply to	
e	to start / to finish	
f	to take	

2 Alicia is talking about her job. Finish what she says with words and phrases from the table above. There can be more than one answer. Be careful with the verbs!

Denke daran!
Das *simple present (she does)* wird verwendet, wenn man über Dinge spricht, die regelmäßig geschehen. Es steht oft zusammen mit den Häufigkeitsadverben *always*, *often* und *sometimes*.

My name is Alicia Kerr and I'm from San Francisco, California. I work for the advertising agency Morgan, Landry & Chavez. I'm a PA and my boss is Mr Landry. I usually **(1)** ____________________ work quite early, at around 7.30. My boss is already here when I arrive – he gets into the office at around 7 o'clock every day. That also means that I can usually **(2)** ____________________ work at around 4 pm, which is nice because I have a small daughter.
My first job each day is to talk to Mr Landry about his diary – the appointments he has and what he has to do that day. After that I do different things all day. I **(3)** __________________ Mr Landry's phone when it rings and put through callers. If Mr Landry isn't in the office when someone calls, I **(4)** __________________ messages to give to him when he gets back. Almost all our correspondence is via email so I have to

(5) ____________________ emails when they come in, and **(6)** ______________________ emails back to people.

There are lots of meetings in advertising agencies and so I often **(7)** ___________________ meetings with Mr Landry and take notes. Clients often visit our offices, too, to talk about their campaigns.

One of the nicest parts of my job is to **(8)** ____________________ visitors when they arrive and to **(9)** ____________________ them until Mr Landry is ready to talk to them.

3 Try this office crossword. All the words were in the unit.

Down

1 a company which does business in many different countries is a … company.
2 a person or company who uses your products or services (*Kunde/Kundin*)
3 *Chef/in*
4 the person in a company who is responsible for selling products (2 words) (*Verkaufsleiter/in*)
6 the plural of the word 'company'
8 the plural of the word 'factory'
14 (v.) to … somebody; (n.) a phone … (*anrufen; Anruf*)

Across

3 a meal in the middle of the day when people discuss business, often in a restaurant (2 words) (*Geschäftsessen*)
5 I work in Germany but my firm's … is in the States. (2 words) (*Hauptsitz*)
6 a place in the USA which is the home of many hi-tech computer companies (2 words)
9 I have to go to a … now. (*Tagung*)
10 abbreviation of 'personal assistant'
11 She is our sales … in Scandinavia. (*Außendienstmitarbeiter/in*)
12 Write the date in my …, please. (*Terminkalender*)
13 a company which transports goods is a … company (*Logistik*)
15 We … our company's business here in Germany. (2 words) (*sich um … kümmern*)

Writing

4 Alicia Kerr (exercise 2) is in a meeting today at her advertising company. She has to write minutes* of the meeting for her boss Mr Landry. You are Alicia. Read what the people say and complete the minutes. Remember to use indirect speech!

Mr Landry (JL)	OK, so that's our new client, a big fruit drinks producer in Florida. Any ideas for TV ads?
Jay Aston (JA)	There are lots of other producers of fruit drinks. I think we need something different from the ordinary ads.
Emily Schnetzer (ES)	I agree. Fruit drinks are always 'healthy' in ads. People see, you know, families in the sunshine, blue sky, …
Ed Robins (ER)	Sure, but that isn't bad. People buy fruit drinks because they're healthy. They compare them with colas and other drinks with lots of sugar.
Jay Aston (JA)	Yes, but 'healthy' doesn't have to mean 'boring'!

Denke daran!
Es gibt noch weitere Wörter neben *to say* und *to tell*, mit denen man die indirekte Rede einleiten kann. Beispiele:
to point out aufzeigen
to suggest vorschlagen
to answer/to reply antworten
to explain erklären
to think glauben, meinen

JL asked for ideas for TV ads for the new client in Florida. JA said that ______________________

____

____

____

____

____

____

____

____

____

Video lounge

5 Videos and films are always good places to learn new words and phrases – which you can then use yourself to make your English more authentic.

1 Watch the video up to the point where Maya and Josh go to the sofa to look at her photos. Tick (✔) the English phrases when you hear them.
2 Write in German meanings for each word or phrase.

on time	rechtzeitig	not to mention	______
Like what?	______	I know what you mean.	______
stuff	______	really nice	______
I guess.	______	Of course not!	______
way too much	______	Time will tell.	______
Really?	______	But enough about …	______

→ *to take minutes: *Protokoll führen*

Anhang

Job pages
Vocabulary by themes

Anhang Job pages

A company profile

A Below you can see see some information from the website of a German company called Weissheimer. Look at the information and answer the questions on the next page in full sentences.

Weissheimer: Welcome to the world of sound

Company name	Weissheimer Electronic GmbH & Co. KG
Headquarters	Hannover, Germany
Company activity	Manufacturer of headphones, microphones and aviation headsets*
Employees	Germany: 1,223 Abroad: 1,103 (Total: 2,326)
History	Founded in 1945 by Dr Karl Weissheimer. The company is still family-owned: the present CEO** is Dr Martin Weissheimer
Turnover (last year)	584.4 million EUR

→ * aviation headset: *Luftfahrt-Headset* → ** CEO (Chief Executive Officer): *Geschäftsführer/in*

1 What is the company's full name.

The company's/Its full name is

2 What product(s) does it make?

3 Where are its headquarters?

4 Who founded the company and when?

5 How much did it earn from the sale of its products last year?

6 How many employees does the company have in total?

7 Of these, how many work in Germany and how many abroad?

8 Which member of the Weissheimer family is the company's CEO at the moment?

9 Where does the company have factories?

10 In how many countries outside Germany does the company have sales offices?

B Do the crossword. All the words are about companies.

Down

1 person who works for a company
2 *in Familienbesitz* (2 words with -)
3 *Hersteller*
6 *Umsatz*

Across

4 *im Ausland*
5 to … = *gründen*
7 *Verkaufsbüro* (2 words)
8 *Fabrik*
9 *weltweit*
10 *Hauptsitz*

Business correspondence 1: an enquiry

1 **You find this magazine article which describes how B2B commerce works. Read the article and choose the best headings for each of the paragraphs 1-4 in the text.**

An order | An enquiry | Finding a new business partner | An offer

How B2B works

B2B stands for Business to Business. We use the expression to talk about commerce between companies – when one company buys something (a product or a service) directly from another company. Think, for example, of a large store. It sells many different goods but it doesn't manufacture them itself. It buys the goods from a manufacturer – in B2B, we call this firm the 'supplier' because it supplies the goods to the store.

(1) ______________________

So, how do two companies first meet and become business partners? There are several different possibilities. We'll call the company which buys the products Company A and the supplier Company B. Company A may see an advertisement from Company B in a trade magazine. These magazines are a good place to look for advertisements for a product you want. Trade fairs are another possibility. At a trade fair, companies show their products and services and there is the chance to talk to the sales people about them. A third possibility is, of course, the internet. Looking online for products is quick and easy – and in today's global world, there is information about companies from around the world.

(2) ______________________

Company A now thinks that it may want to buy a product from Company B. However, before it buys the product it will have some questions and it asks these questions in a letter or email called an 'enquiry'. When we, ordinary consumers, buy something it is relatively easy. We see something we want in a shop or online, we pay the price of the product, and we get it. But B2B commerce is more complicated. Think of the price. In B2B commerce, Company B (the seller) may offer a 'discount' if Company A (the buyer) buys large quantities of the product. Also, the price may include not just the goods but also the cost of transport from the seller to the buyer (who may be in another country). Then again, when must Company A pay for the goods or services – when they order them? when the goods arrive? within a number of days after the goods arrive? These are called the 'terms of payment'. How quickly can Company B supply the goods? And finally, how does Company A know that the goods it buys are, for example, of the quality that they want? Can they first see 'samples' of the goods which they can look at and test for quality? In its enquiry, Company A will ask questions like these.

(3) ______________________________

Company B (the seller) receives Company A's enquiry and it answers the questions in it in an email or letter called an 'offer'. Yes, it can offer a discount. The price includes/doesn't include transport. Company A must pay for the goods when they order them – perhaps later, when Company B knows that Company A always pays efficiently for what it buys, it may offer them the chance to pay within 30 days. Yes, they can send 'samples'.

(4) ______________________________

If Company A (the buyer) is satisfied with Company B's offer, the next step is to buy the goods – to 'place an order'. It often does this with an order form, a special document in which it gives the exact number of goods it wants ('quantities') and the catalogue numbers of the goods so that there are no mistakes. It will also repeat the information that Company B gave in its offer – about discounts, for example – again, so that everything is clear. Finally, when Company B gets the order (and if necessary, the payment for it), it 'dispatches' the goods.

2 Look at the article again and find the English expressions.

1 Dienstleistung ___service___
2 Güter ______________
3 Zulieferfirma ______________
4 zuliefern ______________
5 Hersteller ______________
6 herstellen ______________
7 Geschäftspartner ______________
8 Anzeige/Reklame ______________
9 Fachzeitschrift/Handelsblatt ______________
10 Messe ______________
11 Anfrage ______________
12 Verbraucher/Konsument ______________
13 Preis ______________
14 Rabatt/Preisnachlass ______________
15 innerhalb (einiger Tage) ______________
16 Zahlungsbedingungen ______________
17 Qualität ______________
18 Muster/Proben ______________
19 Angebot ______________
20 einschließen ______________
21 zufrieden sein ______________
22 einen Auftrag erteilen ______________
23 Bestellformular/Auftragsformblatt ______________
24 Katalognummer ______________
25 senden/abfertigen ______________

Business correspondence 2: an offer

1 Read this text about incoterms.

Understanding Incoterms
Incoterms are groups of three letters – for example, CIF - which people in international business use when they buy, sell and transport goods. The letters tell the buyer and the seller exactly what a price includes. CIF means that the price includes the cost of the goods, insurance for the goods when they are transported and the cost of the freight (the transport of the goods). There are 13 incoterms in total. We are going to look at some of the most important. To do this, let us imagine that a manufacturer sells goods to two different buyers in two different countries, Buyer A and Buyer B. You can see the manufacturer and the two buyers in the diagram. The two buyers want to have the goods in their warehouses in their own country.

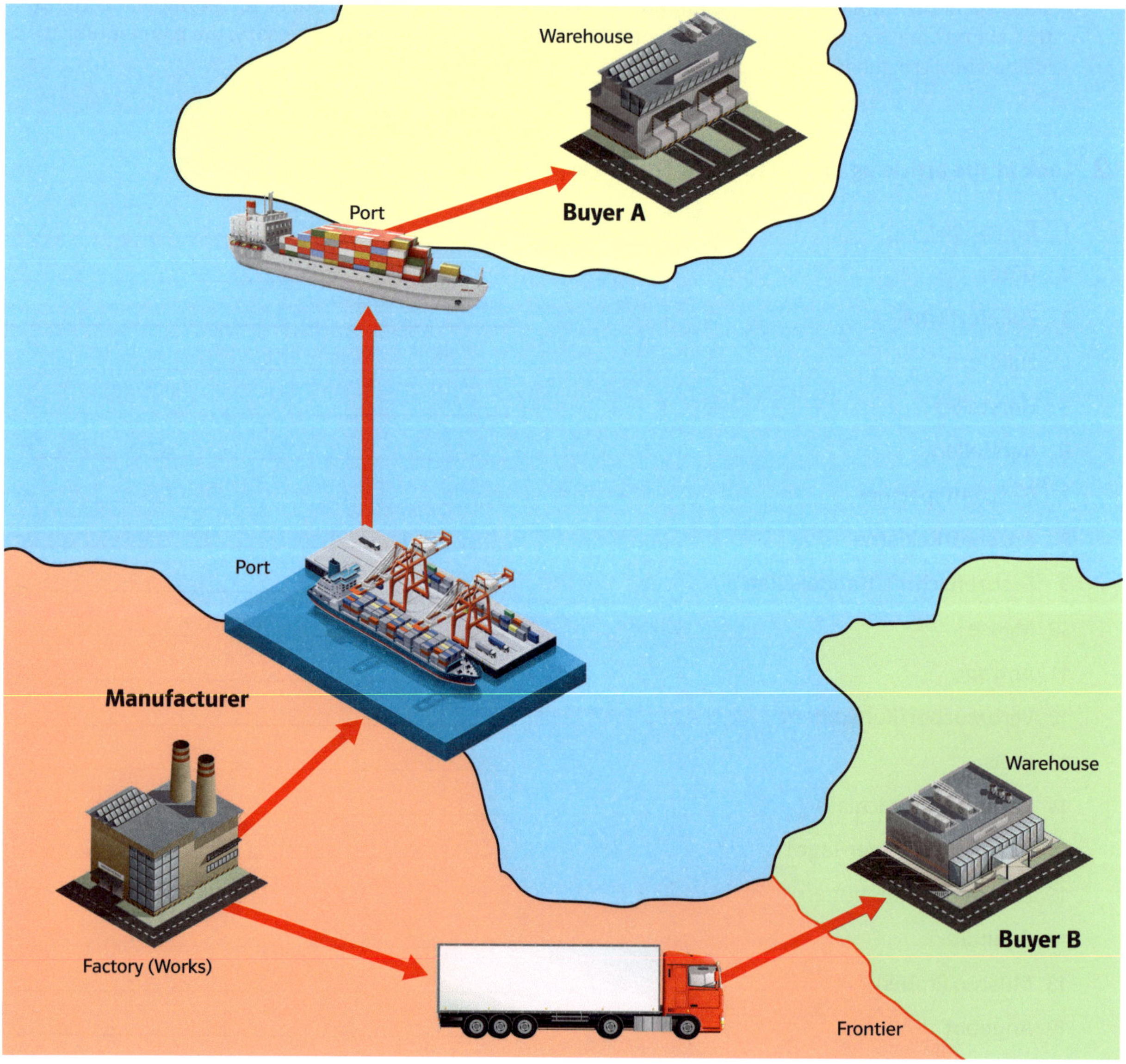

Buyer A
The best way to send the goods to Buyer A is by sea (this is called 'maritime transport'). What different prices are possible? The first, and cheapest, is that Buyer A just pays for the goods themselves – the basic price without transport etc. This is called the 'ex-works' price (EXW). That means the price of the goods as they leave the factory ('works' is another word for factory) and the buyer pays all the transport costs. In German, we call this price *ab Werk*.

Often, however, it is best for the buyer if the manufacturer organises and pays for some or all of the transport. The next possible price, therefore, includes transport to either a port in the manufacturer's country or a port in the buyer's country. Loading and unloading goods at a port also costs money, so buyer and seller need to know if this is included. And insurance is also sometimes included. The following incoterms describe all these possibilities:

- FAS Free Alongside Ship *(frei Längsseite Schiff)* The manufacturer transports the goods to a port in her/his country.
- FOB Free On Board *(frei an Bord)* This time the goods are loaded onto the ship there.
- CFR Cost and Freight *(Kosten und Fracht)* The manufacturer transports the goods to a port in the buyer's country.
- CIF Cost, Insurance and Freight *(Kosten, Versicherung und Fracht)* The same as CFR but the price also includes insurance.
- DEQ Delivered Ex-Quay *(geliefert ab Kai)* The manufacturer also pays to unload the goods in the buyer's port.

With DEQ, the buyer can now collect the goods at a port in her/his country but it is also possible that the manufacturer pays for their transport right to the buyer's warehouse. This price also often includes any taxes ('duty') – a complete service. The incoterm for this is DDP Delivered Duty Paid *(geliefert verzollt)*.

Buyer B

Buyer B is also in another country but the best way to deliver the goods to them is by road (or rail). Again, the buyer can pay just the ex-works price or the price can include everything – the goods are delivered right to the warehouse and the price is again DDP. There are some other possibilities for road and rail transport, too. For example, DAF Delivered At Frontier *(geliefert Grenze)*, where the manufacturer transports the goods to the frontier of the buyer's country. CPT Carriage Paid To *(freifracht bis)* is when the manufacturer transports the goods to a place that the buyer and seller agree on (a railway station, for example).

Incoterms sound complicated but for people in international business, they make life much easier!

2 You are the manufacturer in the diagram on page 54. Calculate the different prices for some goods for Buyer A.

the basic cost of the goods as they leave the factory	transport to the port in your country	loading the goods onto the ship in your country	the journey by sea to the buyer's country	unloading the goods at the port in the buyer's country	transport from the port in the buyer's country to his warehouse plus duty
€1,000	€150	€10	€200	€10	€100

1 The ex-works price: €1,000

2 The FAS price: ______

3 FOB: ______

4 CFR: ______

5 DEQ: ______

6 DDP: ______

Business correspondence 3: an order

1 **Try this business correspondence crossword. All the words were in the Job Pages Business correspondence 1-3 (an enquiry, an offer, an order).**

Down
1 If your prices are … we may want to buy quantities of your products. *(konkurrenzfähig)*
2 *Anfrage*
3 Please send us your … price list. (*aktuell*)
6 (in an email) … is our product catalogue as a pdf document. *(im Anhang)*
7 Please let us know about any … you can offer us. *(Rabatte, pl.)*
8 (at the end of a letter or email) Yours …
9 … order = *Kaufauftrag*
11 We would like … information about your products. *(weitere)*
14 We note that you … payment with our order. *(verlangen, voraussetzen)*
15 Our offer is … for three months. *(gültig)*
17 (1) *Angebot* (2) to … = *anbieten*

Across
4 *Katalog*
5 payment … (*Zahlung in voller Höhe*) (2 words)
9 *Preisliste* (2 words)
10 We have today made a bank … to you of 10,000 euros. (*Überweisung*)
12 The goods will be sent to you within 10 days after … of your order. (*Erhalt, Eingang*)
13 We look … to receiving your order. (*Wir freuen uns auf …*)
16 … discount = *Mengenrabatt*
18 (on a form) (*Gegenstand*)
19 (in a letter) Our order is … (*beiliegend*)

2 **The sentences below are from business letters and emails. In each sentence, a key word is missing. Write in the missing word in each sentence.**

Enquiries

1 We saw your products at the trade fair in Hamburg last week and would like further information.

2 We are a chain of over 30 hotels around Germany. You can find out more about us from our ____________________: www.restaurantzuraltenpfanne…de

3 If your prices are competitive, we may want to buy ____________________ of your products.

4 Please send us you current catalogue and price list. We would also like to know about any ____________________ which you can offer us.

Offers

5 Many thanks for your ____________________ of 21 June.

6 We are pleased to make you the ____________________ offer.

7 Attached are our current catalogue and price list. All our ____________________ are DDP Cologne.

8 We can ____________________ you a volume discount of 5% on all orders over €5,000.

9 For first orders we normally require ____________________ in full with your order.

10 We will ____________________ your goods within five working days of receipt of your order.

11 This offer is ____________________ for six months.

12 Thank you again for your interest in our products and I look forward to receiving your ______________.

Orders

13 Thank you for your ____________________ of 5 December. Please find enclosed our purchase order.

14 We ____________________ that your prices are DEQ Harwich and that you can offer us a 3% volume discount.

15 We also note that for a first order you ____________________ payment with our order and we have today made a bank transfer to your for the price of our goods.

3 **The expressions below are all common in business letters and emails. Match the halves of the expressions.**

1 Dear	a 30 days
2 Yours	b 8 April
3 I look forward to	c catalogue
4 thank you for your letter of	d enclosed/attached
5 product	e list
6 price	f order
7 purchase	g sincerely
8 please find	h Sirs
9 within	i hearing from you soon

Business correspondence 4: a complaint

1 **You find this article about problems which can happen in commerce. Read it and complete the chart below with key words and phrases from the text.**

Mistakes in commerce often have to do with	sending ...
Problem 1:	a delay in ...
Problem 2:	
Problem 3:	
Problem 4:	
A mistake is important but	

PUTTING THINGS RIGHT

Mistakes in business are annoying, but they happen. In commerce, these mistakes often have to do with sending goods.

The first problem that can happen is that the goods don't arrive on time. There is a 'delay in delivery'. For example, the supplier promises to send the goods within ten days. But ten days come and go, and the goods aren't there. Why not? There are a number of possibilities. One may be just a simple mistake by the supplier – a person in the dispatch department of the supplier's company doesn't see the order, for example. But sometimes, there may be a reason for the delay. If the supplier is a manufacturer, it is possible that they have a problem in their factory – with a machine, for example – and can't make the goods. Whatever the reason, a delay in delivery is, of course, a problem for the buyer who needs the goods. The buyer may be a shop, for example, and if it doesn't have the products, it can't sell them.

A second problem that can happen is that the goods arrive, but they are damaged, often because the packaging is not good enough. Imagine, for example, that you order some delicate instruments, or some glass products. If the packaging is not strong, the products inside will get broken. However, it is also possible that the problem is not with the packaging. That may be fine. But the company which transports the packages, the 'carrier', can still damage the goods if it is not careful with them, for example, if the packages are dropped. So again, the problem may not be the fault of the supplier.

Goods which arrive damaged are one of the things that can go wrong in commerce.

A third problem can be another kind of mistake. The supplier sends the wrong goods. You order 500 large T-shirts but your supplier sends you 500 small T-shirts (or 50 large ones instead of 500). In a busy company, this kind of mistake is always possible but again, for the buyer, it is always annoying.

>>

Finally, there is a fourth problem which can happen. Let's say you are a shop again. You buy some goods from your supplier and sell them in your store but soon your customers begin to bring the things they bought back to the shop. They don't work or there are other problems with their quality. What has happened is that some or all of the goods in the consignment were 'faulty' (another word is 'defective'). This may be that your supplier has a quality control problem. However, again, it may be that something just went wrong for a short time in the production department and the problem happens once but never again.

Problems happen but for the supplier the important thing is (s)he must put the problem right. Suppliers need their customers and they don't want to lose them. A mistake is important, but how you put it right is even more important.

2 Below are extracts from four emails. All the emails are complaints. Read the emails and under each one write what kind of problem the writer is complaining about.

Email 1

I'm writing with reference to our order number 1554. The goods arrived yesterday on time as always. However, when we opened the consignment we found that carton no. 6 contained 200 men's polo shirts instead of the 200 women's polo shirts that we had ordered. This is a big problem for us as we are planning a special promotion next week of women's clothing.

Type of problem: ____________________

Email 2

I'm afraid I have to write to you about our order no. K61553. The consignment arrived yesterday. Unfortunately, when we opened the crates we discovered that all the solar panels in one crate (4A) were badly damaged. You must understand that this makes things very difficult for us as we need to install the panels in the next 2-3 days.

Type of problem: ____________________

Email 3

The energy saving light bulbs* which we ordered on the 21 May have still not arrived although you promised to deliver them within two weeks. Unfortunately, this is not the first time that a consignment from you has not arrived on time and if you are not able to send us the bulbs immediately we will have to look for a new supplier.

Type of problem: ____________________

Email 4

I am writing with reference to our order no. PF5151 for 250 ballpoint pens** which we received from you two weeks ago. Unfortunately, a number of our customers have brought back pens and have complained that they do not work. This is very difficult for us as we have a good reputation for the quality of the products which we sell in our stores.

Type of problem: ____________________

→ * energy saving light bulb: *Energiesparlampe* **ballpoint pen: *Kugelschreiber*

Writing an advertisement

This is Luigi Russo. Luigi is from Italy originally but he has lived in Danbury for the last 20 years and he has a pizzeria there: Luigi's Pizzas. Last year, a big, national pizza chain also opened a take-away pizza place in town and now Luigi wants to advertise his pizzas with a flyer. Last week, he contacted an advertising agency and today, he is talking on the phone to Steve Hewett, who works at the agency. Read their conversation and complete the flyer on the next page.

Steve Mr Russo...

Luigi Luigi, please call me Luigi. Everybody calls me Luigi!

Steve OK, er, Luigi. And I'm Steve. You spoke to my colleague Pat Maxwell last week about your advertisement. Well, I have an idea for a flyer now.

Luigi Great!

Steve I'll describe it to you. In the top left-hand corner there's your name, Luigi's Pizzas, and directly under that your slogan. This other pizza firm in town is new, so I want to remind* people that your pizzeria is much older. So the slogan is: 'The best in town since 1995'.

Luigi That's good!

Steve Great. Then in the top right-hand corner there's your address, 'Luigi's Pizzas, 11 Market Place, Danbury', and under that your telephone number. Now, the theme of your flyer is that you deliver your pizzas quickly – much more quickly than the new pizzeria, which is a bit slow at the moment. So under your slogan on the left there's a question in big letters: 'Are you tired of eating cold pizza?' Next to that on the right is a nice cartoon of a pizza chef on a scooter and under the picture the words, again quite big letters, 'We deliver fast!' What do you think so far?

Luigi I like it! Good job, Steve.

Steve Thanks. OK, so then comes the text. The theme is still that people get your pizzas quickly. The text is in three paragraphs. Paragraph one: 'When you order a pizza you want it fast. And hot. But sometimes when it arrives it looks and tastes like an old shoe!'

Luigi Nice!

Steve Paragraph two is: 'Not a Luigi's pizza! If you live in Danbury, we GUARANTEE (that's in capital letters) delivery in 20 minutes OR YOUR MONEY BACK! (in capitals again). That's right. No pizza in 20 minutes and you pay nothing.' And then the third paragraph tells people how to get a pizza: 'Isn't it time you got your pizzas hot? Call us TODAY (capitals) on, then under that in the centre and nice and big so people see it clearly your telephone number again. And finally, at the bottom, your name and your slogan again. They can be in quite big letters again.

Luigi Steve, that's great. Thanks!

Steve No problem. I'll print** one flyer for you and send it over later today.

→ * to remind sb: *jmdn erinnern* → ** to print sth: *etw drucken*

LUIGI'S PIZZAS

(1) ______________________

Luigi's Pizzas

(2) ______________________

(3) ______________________

____

____

____

TELEPHONE: (10299) 414414

(4) ______________________

(5) ______________________

____

____

____

____

____

(6) ______________________

(7) ______________________

Anhang Vocabulary by themes

Vocabulary by themes

On these pages, the most important vocabulary you have learned is arranged by themes. For each theme:

1. write in the German translations of the word or phrase;
2. choose *ten* words or phrases and write an example sentence for each on a separate piece of paper or in your vocabulary notebook.

NOTE: AE = American English; BE = British English.

1 Occupations

Tips and tricks

- Denke daran, immer *a/an* vor Berufsbezeichnungen zu verwenden:
  She is ***a*** *nurse.*
- Verwechsele das englische Wort *chef* nicht mit dem deutschen Wort *Chef/Chefin.*
  A chef works in a kitchen. (Küchenchef)
  My boss is the sales manager. (Chef)

		Schreibe deine eigenen Sätze
admin(istrative) assistant		
architect		
beauty therapist		
businessman/businesswoman		
businessperson/ businesspeople		
call centre worker		
carpenter		
check-in clerk		
chef		
computer games developer		
computer technician		
construction worker		
customs officer		
doctor		
electrician		
factory worker		
farmer		
fashion designer		
film director		
flight attendant		
hairdresser		
hotel receptionist		
inventor		

laboratory technician
lorry driver
make-up artist
manager
marketing assistant
mechanic
mountain rescue worker
nurse
nursery worker
office manager
office worker
painter and decorator
passport officer
personal assistant (PA)
policeman/policewoman
quality control technician
retail (shop) assistant
rugby/football/tennis player
secretary
security officer
shop assistant
teacher
telephone receptionist
tour guide
tradesperson/tradespeople
warehouse worker

2 Companies

Tips and tricks

Denke daran:

- Nach dem Verb *to work* steht *for* in Sätzen wie: *I work **for** a British company.*
- Substantive, die auf Konsonant plus *-y* enden, erhalten im Plural die Endung *-ies*: *company – compan**ies**, factory – factor**ies**, lorry – lorr**ies**, country – countr**ies**.*

Schreibe deine eigenen Sätze

boss (chef = Küchenchef!)
client
customer
department
- marketing (department)
- production
- finance
- logistics
- human resources (HE)
- sales
- research and development (R&D)

employee/employer		
factory		
founder of a company		
global business/company		
globalisation		
goods and services		
head office/headquarters		
history of a company		
laboratory		
local company		
lorry		
manager		
manufacturer		
meeting		
multinational company		
personal assistant (PA)		
producer		
quality control		
raw materials		
retail assistant/shop assistant		
to advertise a product		
to be based in (a place)		
to deliver (a product)		
to found a company		
to grow		
to make/produce/ manufacture a product		
to transport		
turnover (annual sales)		
warehouse		
workplace		

3 Travel

Tips and tricks

Beachte!

- *to go/to travel* ***by*** *bus,* ***by*** *bike,* ***by*** *train,* ***by*** *plane* ***(by*** *air),* ***by*** *ship (****by*** *ferry),* ***by*** *car,* ***by*** *taxi*
- *to go/to walk* ***on*** *foot*

		Schreibe deine eigenen Sätze
abroad		
airport		
arrivals		
(hand) baggage/luggage		
baggage reclaim		
bathroom		

bike/bicycle		
boarding card		
business trip		
check-in clerk		
check-in desk		
country(-ies)		
customs (officer)		
departures		
double room		
duty free (shop)		
facilities (of a hotel)		
first/second floor		
flight		
flight attendant		
gate		
hotel		
key		
lift		
passenger		
passport (control)		
pilot		
plane		
railway station		
registration form		
security check		
shower		
single room		
to arrive		
to board (a plane)		
to book (a room/a flight)		
to depart		
to reserve (a room)		
to take off (plane)		
tram		

4 Starting work

Tips and tricks
Achte auf die Präpositionen:
- *to be good **at** sth*
- *to apply **for** a job*
- *to be interested **in** sth*
- ***at** school, **at** college*

Schreibe deine eigenen Sätze

ability		
advice		
apprentice/apprenticeship		

career
certificate
clothes
co-worker/colleague
CV (curriculum vitae)
date of birth
education
enthusiastic
first day at work
free time
full-time/part-time job
hours of work
interest(s)
interview/interviewer
job advertisement
knowledge of English
letter of application
opportunity
pay
personal details
primary school
qualification
reliable
secondary school
skill
subject (at school)
to advertise (a job)
to answer (a question)
to apply for a job
to ask (a question)
to be good at sth
to be interested in sth
to choose (a career)
to contact sb
to decide (to do sth)
to earn (money)
to get on (well) with (people)
to learn (to do sth)
to leave school/college
to like/love/enjoy doing sth
to promise (to do sth)
to solve (a problem)
to start work
to study
trainee/traineeship
uniform
wage
work experience

working conditions

workplace

5 Commerce

Tips and tricks

Für Geschäftsbriefe ist es hilfreich, wenn man einzelne Wörter nicht isoliert, sondern gleich in einem längeren Ausdruck lernt. Zum Beispiel wird das Wort *enclosed* oft in folgendem Ausdruck verwendet: *Please find enclosed …* Wenn man gleich die komplette Wendung lernt, kann man sie direkt in E-Mails und Geschäftsbriefen benutzen.

		Schreibe deine eigenen Sätze
(business) correspondence		
attachment/attached (to an email)		
bank transfer		
business partner		
business to business (B2B)		
commerce		
competitive		
(to make a) complaint		
consignment		
consumer		
container		
container ship		
cost of transport		
crate		
customer		
damaged		
delay in delivery		
discount		
enclosed (with a letter)		
enquiry		
export department		
ex-works price		
faulty (defective)		
freight		
further (information)		
good will		
incoterms		
insurance		
international trade		
offer		
order		
order form		

packaging		
payment (in full)		
price (of a product)		
price list		
product catalogue		
quantity		
replacement(s)		
sample (of a product)		
terms of payment		
to apologise		
to buy sth/buyer		
to complain		
to dispatch (an order)		
to include		
to load/unload goods		
to make a mistake		
to offer sb sth		
to order		
to place an order		
to receive (noun: receipt)		
to require		
to sell sth/seller		
to supply sth/supplier		
trade fair		
trade magazine		
valid		
within (30 days)		
wrong goods		

6 Useful words and phrases

Tips and tricks

Es ist hilfreich, Wörter gleich in Wortfamilien zu lernen, d.h. Verben, Nomen (und manchmal auch Adjektive), die zusammengehören. Beispiele:

- *to decide (v.) – decision (n.)*
- *to deliver (v.) – delivery (n.)*
- *possible (adj.) – possibility (n.)*

		Schreibe deine eigenen Sätze
1 Verbs		
to assemble (a product)		
to believe		
to borrow sth		
to change sth		
to check sth		
to choose		

to decide
to deliver sth
to describe sth
to discover (a country)
to drive (a car)
to expect
to explain
to fill in (a form)
to forget
to give advice
to grow (= get bigger)
to grow (e.g. tomatoes)
to imagine
to improve sth
to introduce sb
to last (two years)
to lend sb sth
to make sure (that)
to practise
to promise
to remember sth/to do sth
to reply (to sth)
to speak (English)
to speak to sb
to spend (money)
to spend (time)
to stay (at a hotel)
to store (goods in a warehouse)
to succeed
to take/do an exam
to talk (to sb/on the phone)
to translate
to try (to do sth)
to visit (a city/company)
to walk
to wear (clothes)
to worry

2 Adjectives

accurate
amazing
automatic
available
brilliant
careful
comfortable
confident

current
dangerous
different
difficult
efficient
exciting
expensive
famous
foreign
friendly
funny
important
impossible
necessary
popular
possible
reliable
responsible
separate
serious
strange
stupid
successful

3 Useful phrases

first/then/next/after that/ finally
I can't stand
I don't mind
I've lived her for two years.
I've lived here since last May
it depends
nice/pleased to meet you (too)
on the first/second floor
please find attached/enclosed
please note that
Thanks very much. – You're welcome.
that's right
three years ago
to be good/bad at sth
to do an apprenticeship
to go to college
to leave school/college
to make a mistake
to travel by train/by bus/by plane
what sorts(s) of ...?

Notizen

Bildquellennachweis

Cover Thinkstock (Eyecandy Images), München; **3** shutterstock (Anton Gvozdikov), New York, NY; **3** shutterstock (Semmick Photo), New York, NY; **3** Thinkstock (istock/Chanstarco), München; **3** shutterstock (zstock), New York, NY; **3** Thinkstock (Istock/Edsel Querini), München; **3** iStockphoto (ooyoo), Calgary, Alberta; **3** dreamstime.com (Monkey Business Images), Brentwood, TN; **3** Thinkstock (Blend Images/Colin Anderson), München; **3** shutterstock (Monkey Business Images), New York, NY; **7** shutterstock (Anton Gvozdikov), New York, NY; **8** Klett-Archiv, Stuttgart; **9** iStockphoto (clu), Calgary, Alberta; **11** BigStockPhoto.com (Yuri Arcurs), Davis, CA; **11** shutterstock (Semmick Photo), New York, NY; **12** shutterstock (Margaret Smeaton), New York, NY; **12** iStockphoto (Steve Geer), Calgary, Alberta; **12** iStockphoto (fotomy), Calgary, Alberta; **14** dreamstime.com (Modfos), Brentwood, TN; **14** Thinkstock (istock/Chanstarco), München; **14** iStockphoto (Mike_Coles), Calgary, Alberta; **20** shutterstock (Diego Cervo), New York, NY; **21** shutterstock (zstock), New York, NY; **23** Klett-Archiv, Stuttgart; **24** Thinkstock (Istock/Edsel Querini), München; **24** shutterstock (JoLin), New York, NY; **24** Mauritius Images (Alamy), Mittenwald; **24** Avenue Images GmbH (Corbis RF), Hamburg; **25** creativ collection Verlag GmbH, Freiburg; **25** Fotolia.com (Margaret M Stewart), New York; **25** iStockphoto (lucato), Calgary, Alberta; **25** iStockphoto (Jon Helgason), Calgary, Alberta; **29** shutterstock (Danomyte), New York, NY; **30** BigStockPhoto.com (Sonyae), Davis, CA; **30** iStockphoto (ooyoo), Calgary, Alberta; **30** iStockphoto (Windzepher), Calgary, Alberta; **33** Klett-Archiv, Stuttgart; **34** shutterstock (Monkey Business Images), New York, NY; **34** iStockphoto (RUSSELLTATEdotCOM), Calgary, Alberta; **36** iStockphoto (olgna), Calgary, Alberta; **38** shutterstock (PathDoc), New York, NY; **39** iStockphoto (IndigoBetta), Calgary, Alberta; **39** shutterstock (Oceania), New York, NY; **40** shutterstock (Blend Images), New York, NY; **41** Thinkstock (Blend Images/Colin Anderson), München; **44** shutterstock (Lavaria Ferreri Liotti), New York, NY; **44** iStockphoto (Imageegaml), Calgary, Alberta; **44** iStockphoto (sandoclr), Calgary, Alberta; **46** dreamstime.com (Monkey Business Images), Brentwood, TN; **49** iStockphoto (Kyoshino), Calgary, Alberta; **50** iStockphoto (Kupicoo), Calgary, Alberta; **50** iStockphoto (1001nights), Calgary, Alberta; **50** iStockphoto (Mihajlo Maricic), Calgary, Alberta; **50** iStockphoto (Bamlou), Calgary, Alberta; **52** shutterstock (Deklofenak), New York, NY; **53** shutterstock (Dudarev Mikhail), New York, NY; **54** Fotolia.com (Taras Livyy), New York; **54** shutterstock (Alex Mit), New York, NY; **54** Fotolia.com (mallinka1), New York; **54** shutterstock (TheVectorminator), New York, NY; **56** shutterstock (Goodluz), New York, NY; **58** shutterstock (GWImages), New York, NY; **60** Fotolia.com (WavebreakMediaMicro), New York; **61** Fotolia.com (Jokatoons), New York; **62** shutterstock (Racorn), New York, NY; **63** shutterstock (Mubus7), New York, NY; **64** shutterstock (Bernhard Richter), New York, NY; **65** shutterstock (Africa Studio), New York, NY; **67** shutterstock (Jeanette Dietl), New York, NY; **68** Fotolia.com (Momius), New York

Sollte es in einem Einzelfall nicht gelungen sein, den korrekten Rechteinhaber ausfindig zu machen, so werden berechtigte Ansprüche selbstverständlich im Rahmen der üblichen Regelungen abgegolten.